T0198605

Writing
BLOCKBUSTER
Plots

A STEP-BY-STEP GUIDE TO MASTERING PLOT, STRUCTURE & SCENE

Martha Alderson

BESTSELLING AUTHOR OF *THE PLOT WHISPERER*

Writing BLOCKBUSTER Plots

WRITER'S DIGEST
BOOKS

Writer's Digest Books
An imprint of Penguin Random House LLC
penguinrandomhouse.com

ISBN 978-1-59963-979-6

Edited by Rachel Randall
Designed by Alexis Estoye

ACKNOWLEDGMENTS

I owe a big debt of gratitude to all of the writers that openly shared their need, and often desperation for and resistance to, plot and structure and scene. I may never have self-published the original *Blockbuster Plots* if not for them, which would never have led to *The Plot Whisper* and best-selling author status. I know for a fact that *A Spiritual Guide for Writers: Secrets of Personal Transformation* would have remained hidden and unrealized.

I continue to give thanks to Teresa LeYung Ryan and Luisa Adams for their love, generosity, and belief in me. Added gratitude goes to Luisa for her gentle and nurturing nature and a shared belief in the healing power of spirit.

Thanks also to the following:

Melanie Rigney for being the first person to believe in my approach to teaching writers how to plot, and for believing in me. Thank you for your encouragement when I needed it most.

Phil Sexton for his patience and his offer to breathe freshness into the original *Blockbuster Plots*, which has sent me on a twelve-year journey into the heart of stories, writers, and me.

Rachel Randall for taming what often felt like chaos, editing with a brilliant eye for detail, and caring for and vastly improving *Blockbuster Plots*. Cris Freese for seamlessly stepping in with his support.

Writer's Digest for their endorsement from the very beginning. Thank you for finding merit in my work as early as 2003.

There are many to thank in the intervening years between the first *Blockbuster Plots* and what *Writing Blockbuster Plots* is today, including the University of Santa Cruz Extension, the California Writers Club, Brian Parker, various writers' groups, the San Francisco Writing Conference, Jill Corcoran, Adams Media, Peter Archer, Paula Munier, and Jordan Rosenfeld.

I am forever grateful to my husband, Bobby Ray Alderson, for his love and protection, for never letting up on me to finish as I labored to bring my original vision of *Blockbuster Plots* into form, and for his constant and passionate belief in me.

ABOUT THE AUTHOR

MARTHA ALDERSON is known as the Plot Whisperer for her books on plot: *The Plot Whisperer: Secrets of Story Structure Any Writer Can Master*, *The Plot Whisperer Workbook: Step-by-Step Exercises to Help You Create Compelling Stories*, *The Plot Whisperer Book of Writing Prompts: Easy Exercises to Get You Writing*, and *Writing Deep Scenes: Plotting Your Story Through Action, Emotion, and Theme* (with Jordan Rosenfeld), and for the award-winning blog she manages, *The Plot Whisperer*, which has been awarded top honors by *Writer's Digest* from 2009 to 2015.

Martha has been exploring and writing about the Universal Story for the past twenty years as part of the plot support she offers to writers. More recently, she has expanded her work to include helping writers transform their creative lives.

She is currently filming two new video programs: *The 27-Step Tutorial: How Do I Plot a Novel, Memoir, Screenplay?* and *A Spiritual Guide for Writers: Secrets of Personal Transformation.*

Visit her website: marthaalderson.com

TABLE OF CONTENTS

PART ONE: PLOT PLANNER

PART TWO: SCENE TRACKER

PART THREE: APPENDICES

INTRODUCTION
TO THE
REVISED EDITION

Before self-publishing *Blockbuster Plots: Pure & Simple* (BBP) in 2003, I searched the index of every popular writing book I could get my hands on. If I did find mention of plot, I never found more than a single chapter. At that time, the focus of these books was on writing for discovery. Plot and structure constricted the channels for creativity and stifled inspiration. I found the opposite to be true with my students: Structure doesn't kill creativity. Rather, developing fixed boundaries enables creativity, sparking innovation and freeing the mind of the tension of aimless wandering. Since then there has been an explosion of books on plot. Currently, plot is mentioned, discussed, and taught in every writing circle, for every genre, and using a variety of approaches.

Now it's time to go back to the basics. Early on, I found that writers instinctively know that they can immediately improve their stories with a command of plot, structure, and scene. Falling back on a commonly recognized mantra for writers (and my experience in special education), I strived to *show* plot, structure, and the essential elements of scene with the help of two visual templates I developed, the Plot Planner and Scene Tracker, instead of *telling* or lecturing on these elusive elements. But as much as some writers wanted help, they were also resistant and fearful of organized, linear templates. Even when some writers fought back, I persisted. I wanted writers to experience the freedom of structure—I saw that *ah-ha* moment flash across too many writers' faces. These writers benefited from facing their fears, trying new techniques, and finding solutions to problems in their writing that they didn't know existed. I encouraged writers to lean on plot, structure, and scene concepts because I received e-mails and handwritten letters from other writers, expressing their thanks.

The longer I taught plot to writers, the more stories, memoirs, and screenplays I analyzed for common, universal elements of plot, structure, and scene. At the same time, I gained insight into writers' inner worlds of creativity. From this exploration and insight, I developed self-produced plot workshop DVDs (now online video programs), the Plot Whisperer blog, and *The Plot Whisperer*, my first traditionally published book. In *The Plot Whisperer*, I introduced the idea of the Universal Story—a concept of birth, growth, death, and renewal that exists at the core of every narrative (and of life itself). That turned me into a best-selling author.

Throughout the years, as writing trends shift and as I delve deeper into the secrets of change and transformation based on the Universal Story, I've stayed true to every single idea in *Writing Blockbuster Plots*. But I've also expanded on my original ideas, always returning to the two templates I offer here: the Plot Planner and the Scene Tracker. These visual representations of plot and scene remain at the core of my work. They even translate to transformation for writers and people interested in living a more fulfilling life.

Martha Alderson
Santa Cruz, California
September 2015

INTRODUCTION

Are you confused about plot? You are not alone. Plot took me years to pin down. I attended all sorts of writing workshops but found much of the information difficult to transfer to the page. I read all sorts of books on the craft of writing, but the advice generally boiled down to putting your character in a pickle and seeing what happens next. This technique works for many successful writers, but it did not work for me.

I longed for something more concrete—not a formula per se, but specific guidelines to help bring depth to my storylines. I searched for anything I could find that directly addressed the issue of plot development. Unable to find what I sought, I berated myself for not grasping what everyone else seemed to understand naturally. I even quit writing for a spell, reasoning that if I were truly meant to be a writer, it would come more easily for me. But the muse continued to haunt me. Over time, I came to realize that everyone else was struggling with plot; they just were not talking about it.

Through years of perseverance and determination, I pinned down the elusive concept of plot to the point where I could actually "see" it. Wanting to save others the frustration I had experienced, and using what I know about how people learn, I started teaching plot to writers. *Writing Blockbuster Plots* was born of that passion.

In workshops and private consultations, I have witnessed what happens when writers delve more deeply into the dynamics of cause and effect. If you explore how well-constructed characters in conflict act as the driving force behind an exceptional story, you will be better able to create your own exceptional stories. Explore the themes of your own life, and your projects will have lasting meaning.

The techniques I offer in *Writing Blockbuster Plots* have helped thousands of writers create dramatic action plots, and heighten tension and suspense in scenes as well as in the overall story.

Plot is a series of scenes arranged by cause and effect to create dramatic action filled with tension and conflict that furthers the character's emotional development and creates thematic significance.

WHO THIS BOOK IS FOR

If you are having a difficult time seeing where your story is headed, or if ideas are rolling around in your head but you are having trouble getting started, or if your book has been rejected time and time again, you most likely need help with plot. This is the book for you.

Whether you are a screenwriter, a memoirist, or an author of children's, young adult, or adult fiction, you will benefit from a firm understanding of scene and a concrete method for developing a plotline that combines the dramatic action, character emotional development, and thematic elements of your project.

Devising a clearly formulated plotline helps authors get going, prevents them from stalling partway through, and guarantees that even those who typically never finish anything will make it to the end.

When this book calls for interactive participation, I encourage you to do so using your own characters and scenes. If you have not yet started a writing project, use your imagination or a book by your favorite author.

Use *Writing Blockbuster Plots* in conjunction with one of my online writing workshop video programs[1] or on its own. Either way, the techniques presented here will change your writing life forever. For the sake of convenience, this book gives independent consideration to the dramatic action, character emotional development, and thematic significance of a story. But keep in mind that all aspects of a successful story must become integrated to create unity. Achieving this unity is the goal of every writer.

---

1 Access these videos at marthaalderson.com/video-courses.

HOW TO USE THIS BOOK

Writing Blockbuster Plots is divided into two parts: Plot Planner and Scene Tracker. Both parts are step-by-step, interactive guides for providing depth for your stories and maximizing the impact of your scenes.

Your ability to plot is strengthened by doing the work.

The Plot Planner

Plot springs from a character in conflict. The Plot Planner is a storyboard that shows how the three essential plots—dramatic action, character emotional development, and thematic meaning—rise and fall together from beginning to end. You will learn about action, character, and thematic plot using your scene and story ideas to create a Plot Planner for your latest project.

The next several pages contain an example of a Plot Planner for the suspense novel *Folly* by award-winning author Laurie R. King. The protagonist, Rae Newborn, is a woman teetering on the edge of sanity and reeling from tragedy. She moves to Folly Island to restore the home of her mysterious great-uncle and to rebuild her life, but she must battle her own paranoia and "watchers" in the trees—who may or may not be a figment of her imagination.

We will return to the beginning, middle, and end sections of this Plot Planner throughout Part One.

Folly by Laurie R. King

This Plot Planner uses symbols to indicate scenes that show character emotional development (≈) and dramatic action (◊).

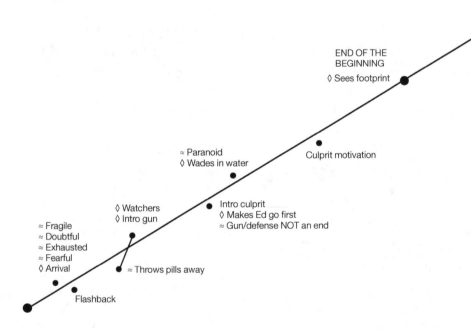

END OF THE
BEGINNING
◊ Sees footprint

Culprit motivation

≈ Paranoid
◊ Wades in water

◊ Watchers
◊ Intro gun

Intro culprit
◊ Makes Ed go first
≈ Gun/defense NOT an end

≈ Fragile
≈ Doubtful
≈ Exhausted
≈ Fearful
◊ Arrival

≈ Throws pills away

Flashback

THE MIDDLE
(½)

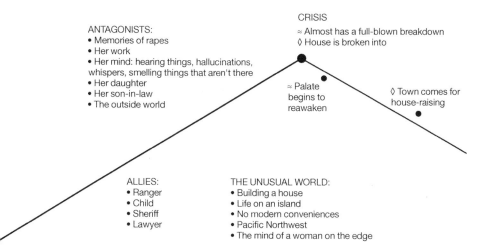

CRISIS

ANTAGONISTS:
- Memories of rapes
- Her work
- Her mind: hearing things, hallucinations, whispers, smelling things that aren't there
- Her daughter
- Her son-in-law
- The outside world

≈ Almost has a full-blown breakdown
◊ House is broken into

≈ Palate begins to reawaken

◊ Town comes for house-raising

ALLIES:
- Ranger
- Child
- Sheriff
- Lawyer

THE UNUSUAL WORLD:
- Building a house
- Life on an island
- No modern conveniences
- Pacific Northwest
- The mind of a woman on the edge

KEY
≈ Character Emotional Development
◊ Dramatic Action

Download a larger version of this Plot Planner at
www.writersdigest.com/writing-blockbuster-plots.

THE END
(¼)

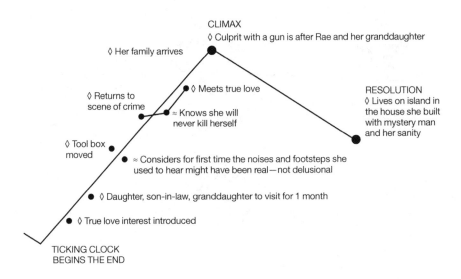

CLIMAX
◊ Culprit with a gun is after Rae and her granddaughter

◊ Her family arrives

◊ Meets true love

◊ Returns to
scene of crime

RESOLUTION
◊ Lives on island in
the house she built
with mystery man
and her sanity

≈ Knows she will
never kill herself

◊ Tool box
moved

≈ Considers for first time the noises and footsteps she
used to hear might have been real—not delusional

● ◊ Daughter, son-in-law, granddaughter to visit for 1 month

● ◊ True love interest introduced

TICKING CLOCK
BEGINS THE END

KEY
≈ Character Emotional Development
◊ Dramatic Action

Download a larger version of this Plot Planner at
www.writersdigest.com/writing-blockbuster-plots.

The Scene Tracker

A good scene advances the plot of the story, develops the character, contributes to the theme, provides tension and conflict, and/or reflects a change in emotion or circumstances. A great scene does all of these things at once. The Scene Tracker is a form that helps you see all of the important layers of each of your scenes side by side and step by step from the beginning to the end of your project.

This is an example of a Scene Tracker that shows three important scenes from the coming-of-age middle-grade novel *Tracker* by award-winning author Gary Paulsen. In this story, a young boy begins to believe that a deer he has been tracking for two days has the power to cheat death and save the life of his grandfather, who is dying of cancer.

Scene Tracker: *Tracker* by Gary Paulsen

NOTES: Thematic Significance: "Beauty comes from instinct and helps you remember."

SCENE (SC) OR SUMMARY (SU)	TIME AND SETTING	CHARACTER EMOTIONAL DEVELOPMENT	GOAL	DRAMATIC ACTION	CONFLICT	CHANGE IN EMOTION	THEMATIC DETAILS
The Beginning (1/4)							
SC: End of the Beginning	Wednesday night The field Nov./cold	Writes poetry Talks to Grandfather about poetry	To clean out manure pile	Deer sighting	X	+/+/-	Beauty comes from instinct
The Middle (1/2)							
SC: Crisis	Noon The woods	Uses the rifle instinctually "The deer knows me" and he knows her	Get the doe early	Unable to shoot	X	He is determined, which changes to apprehensive when he recognizes the deer, which changes to his inability to shoot	By not shooting, he holds back death
The End (1/4)							
SC: Climax	The next day 1 p.m. The woods	Crawls on hands and knees	To touch the deer	Touches deer	X	+/-/-	He had won = life taken from death

What You Need

Throughout *Writing Blockbuster Plots*, you are invited to apply the techniques to your own work or, if you don't currently have a work-in-progress, to use the work of a writer you admire. I encourage you to use your own work, no matter how rough you believe it is. Either way, all you need to proceed are the following:

- a willing heart
- a copy of your manuscript or a book that you do not mind marking up
- a six-foot strip of banner paper
- a set of markers
- a pad of sticky notes

If your heart is willing but your mind recoils from the methodical, organized approach to the creative process presented in this book, I encourage you to step out of your comfort zone. One resistant writer moaned that she was not an organized person and that these techniques would not work for her. Yet she knew her story needed help, so she stuck with it. Now she encourages other resistant writers to remain open to practices they may find valuable, and to confront their fears and grow as writers.

If you like to work things out on the page, so be it. But at the same time, consider the ideas in this book. A key element in the nature of creativity is giving yourself time to work things out. When you are ready for your first rewrite, perhaps then you will be ready to give the techniques a try.

SENSORY FEEDBACK

In my life before writing, I founded a speech, language, and learning disability clinic for children and young adults. For more than twenty years, I interacted with thousands of children and came to appreciate firsthand the many different ways people learn.

In appreciation for all the different styles of learning that exist, *Writing Blockbuster Plots* is formatted to provide you with as much sensory feedback as possible for full discovery and for ease in learning. The more you actively participate in the process, the more you will grasp. The idea is to shake things up. Do things differently and watch your piece rush at you in a completely new way.

This book is divided between hands-on activities and corresponding explanations. A pencil icon will notify you of each "hands-on" step toward creating your own Plot Planner and Scene Tracker. I also provide straightforward explanations that will appeal to your cognition. Each time you fill in a form, your sense of touch is stimulated and gives you kinesthetic feedback.

One sense I cannot provide on these pages is the sense of hearing. If at any point in the book you lose your energy or passion for further exploration into your writing, or if you are confronted with something that feels uncomfortably challenging, read the passages aloud. You may find that you benefit from the auditory feedback.

As a result of all my years of teaching, I have found that it is easier to welcome new material when we stay open and loose. Therefore, I suggest you breathe and do what you have to do to remain relaxed. We have all been taught to try harder when confronting a challenge. But actually, the harder we try, the tenser we become, closing off our ability to absorb and assimilate new information. I've included reminders throughout the book to prompt you to stop every so often to take a moment to reflect and relax.

EXAMPLES

Throughout both parts of *Writing Blockbuster Plots*, I provide you with examples of how other writers successfully accomplished the tasks offered. The examples are intended to empower you.

Many of the examples are from Pulitzer Prize–winning fiction. Let me assure you that I did not choose these brilliant examples of plot and scene to intimidate you. Rather, I use them with the firm belief that the stories came to their authors just as your story comes to you: through a lot of hard work and many rewrites.

The exploration into plot and scene will ensure that with each rewrite you will give your story a sharper focus and greater depth.

WHAT TO EXPECT

If you are an intuitive writer who likes to find your way on the page, you may feel overwhelmed or balk at some of the techniques offered in this book. Go ahead and acknowledge the resistance. Then find a way to make the system work for you. The ideas presented here are left-brained activities. You likely feel more comfortable working with the right side of your brain. However, these techniques will support your intuitive side by defining boundaries in which you can create. This process will ultimately help your writing. What I offer here can and should be revised in any way that serves your writing.

Symbols are posted along the way to help facilitate learning. For example, there is a lightbulb icon in the middle of chapter three. For those of you who benefit from immediate, experiential, hands-on learning, this is a spot where you can put this book down and pick up your own project. If you choose to pause at the lightbulbs, go ahead and try out the technique and organization until you are ready to move on.

If at any point while you are working on the techniques offered in *Writing Blockbuster Plots* you feel inspired to return to the actual writing of your story, by all means put this book down and do so.

Remember: The ideas offered in *Writing Blockbuster Plots* are not rules; they are simply loose guidelines intended to be bent, ignored, and adapted in whatever way best supports your storytelling.

part one
PLOT PLANNER

PLOTTING
IS LIKE
JUGGLING

Imagine yourself as a juggler, and you are juggling one ball. For our purposes, we will label this first ball "dramatic action."

Toss this first ball in the air. It is best to "pop" the ball from the palm of your hand rather than to let it roll off your fingertips. This metaphor also applies to plotting out your stories: It is best to start with a "pop" of dramatic action rather than to let your story unfold at a leisurely pace. Also, it is best not to throw the ball too high—in other words, you don't want to introduce too much dramatic action too soon. With the help of the Plot Planner, you'll see how the intensity of a story builds incrementally from beginning to end, and you will also learn how to create smooth transitions from one scene to the next without letting the action drift.

With the dramatic action ball in play, it is time to integrate ball two. This one we label "character emotional development." As the action ball starts to descend toward your hand again, pop the character ball in the air. This means that when the tension or conflict or suspense caused by the dramatic action starts to fall or lose its effect, you can use your character's emotional development, his flaw or prejudice or fears, to cause more.

What message do you want your reader left with after reading the story? This will be ball three, "thematic significance."

As in real juggling, when one ball or layer of plot falls and its conflict and tension is reduced, another element of plot is sent airborne, and its conflict and tension increases. As you become confident with these three balls or layers of plot, you can add more: the subplots of secondary characters, history or politics, and so on. The more you practice, the better you will become, until you are tossing the balls while standing on one foot with your eyes closed. Eventually you may even be able to juggle knives and mallets and the kitchen sink.

Like a juggler, the more adept you are at keeping all three elements of plot rising and falling through cause and effect, the deeper, richer, and more compelling your story.

THE PLOT PLANNER

The Plot Planner is a visual tool to help you keep an eye on your story as a whole as you write its individual parts made up of scenes and summaries.

Practice alone will not turn all of us into jugglers. Some of us do better when the steps are mapped out on paper. In the case of plotting, think of the Plot Planner as the route or map of the journey you envision for your protagonist. Along this route, the three elements of plot—the dramatic action, the character's emotional development, and thematic significance—will rise and fall.

When you start planning your plot, your route will likely contain lots of gaps and dead ends, but these will be smoothed over and filled in as you come to know your story and characters better.

Once the plan is in place on your Plot Planner and you and your protagonist have set off, one of you is likely to trip up or misread the map or even intentionally veer off the planned route. Stay loose, but try to keep close to the plan as the dramatic action sends your character off a cliff or crashing through the underbrush to slay a dragon or two before fighting her way to the top peak. Puffing hard, you reach the summit together. Oops, it's not the summit after all. A crisis ensues. The true summit shimmers in the distance. In a rush of energy and excitement, you scramble alongside your character toward the final struggle, the climax of the book.

I recommend building your Plot Planner horizontally, on big pieces of banner paper taped to the wall. This serves as a continual visual reminder of your entire story and helps you keep the larger picture in your mind as you concentrate on smaller parts: writing and rewriting chapters and scenes, creating just the right sentence, choosing just the right word.

If you do not have the space available or simply are not inclined to wallpaper your walls with story ideas, then use smaller paper. Or, if you are adept at keeping all of these ideas in your head at once without the visual support, plan your story with a spreadsheet on your computer. Use whatever method encourages you to actually write. Find a way that works for you.

It can be tough to simultaneously juggle all three primary and intertwining plot threads, plus the countless other plot elements. Often we end up trying too hard. Our writing suffers, and we become stiff and self-conscious. The joy of writing diminishes. If you are struggling with keeping all the balls in the air at once, try following one thread at a time. Rather than outline your plot in list form or storyboard your ideas in a flat and linear progression, you can plot scenes and scene ideas on a Plot Planner. One plotline at a time, follow the rise and fall in the same dynamic pattern found in all great stories.

As you plot action scenes, remember the primary reason people go to the movies and read books is for the characters. Jot down ideas, pin character and setting images to your wall, or add a historic time line to a Plot Planner. With one plotline either vaguely or firmly in place, weave the character's emotional development in and out of the external excitement. The more you write and the more interactive you are with your Plot Planner board, the more thoroughly the overall meaning of the story, as well as the meaning in each scene, will emerge.

Plot one plot thread on a Plot Planner at a time or all three simultaneously—you choose.

Again, there are no rules when it comes to writing fiction. Every idea I present has as many exceptions as rules. Every Pulitzer Prize–winning example I cite can be matched by a Pulitzer Prize–winning example that illustrates the opposite.

Now you are ready to develop the map for your story using the Plot Planner.

Chapter One

WHAT IS PLOT?

This is an example of what plot is *not*: "The king dies. The queen dies."

This is an example of what plot *is*: "The king dies, and then the queen dies of grief." [1]

What distinguishes the first example from the second? Sure, the first example tells the reader what happens and carries a certain dramatic flair because it involves death. It has *dramatic action* (the death) but no *character emotional development* and no *thematic significance*. Furthermore, "The king dies. The queen dies," is episodic—there is no linkage between the two events, no *cause and effect*.

The second example demonstrates plot. That the queen dies from her grief over the king's death signifies character emotional development. We can extract from this the thematic significance: Love kills. Lastly, the two events demonstrate cause and effect, because they are linked by causality. In other words, the king's death is the cause, and the queen's grief—and ultimately her death—is the effect.

These examples beautifully illustrate the following definition of plot:

> Plot is a series of SCENES that are deliberately arranged by CAUSE AND EF-FECT to create DRAMATIC ACTION filled with TENSION AND CONFLICT to further the CHARACTER'S EMOTIONAL DEVELOPMENT and provide THEMATIC SIGNIFICANCE.

---

1 This example comes from novelist E.M. Forster.

SIFTING THROUGH THE LAYERS

This definition is complicated. Let's study each layer of the definition, signified by the capitalized words.

Scenes

> Plot is a series of SCENES ...

We cover scene in depth in Part Two of this book with the help of the Scene Tracker template. For now, simply appreciate that plot comes alive in the moment-by-moment action shown in scene, not in summary.

Cause and Effect

> Plot is a series of *scenes* that are deliberately arranged by CAUSE AND EFFECT ...

"Cause and effect" means that each scene comes directly out of the scene that came before it. In other words, one scene causes the next scene. This creates a satisfying story for readers, because each scene is organic: From the seeds you plant in the first scene, the next scene emerges.

Chapter six discusses cause and effect in depth.

Dramatic Action

> Plot is a series of *scenes* that are deliberately arranged by *cause and effect* to create DRAMATIC ACTION ...

The dramatic meaning comes from the action scenes, which are scenes that are played out moment by moment on the page through action and dialogue. Drama is created when the reader is uncertain about the outcome of a scene and the answer to the dramatic question—will or won't the character succeed?

Chapter eight provides a plan for the dramatic action of your piece.

Tension and Conflict

> Plot is a series of *scenes* that are deliberately arranged by *cause and effect* to create *dramatic action* filled with TENSION AND CONFLICT ...

Tension is present in any scene in which the protagonist is not in control. An outside force preventing her from moving forward creates conflict. Scenes with conflict, tension, suspense, and curiosity are dramatic and compel a reader to turn the pages faster.

Chapter nine gives you a visual idea of how tension and conflict affect the overall plot of your story.

Character Emotional Development

> Plot is a series of *scenes* that are deliberately arranged by *cause and effect* to create *dramatic action* filled with *tension and conflict* to further the CHARACTER'S EMOTIONAL DEVELOPMENT ...

Emotional meaning always comes from your characters. Character emotional development shows the effect the dramatic action has on the character over time throughout the story.

Chapter twelve demonstrates how character emotional development interweaves with the dramatic action.

Thematic Significance

> Plot is a series of *scenes* that are deliberately arranged by *cause and effect* to create *dramatic action* filled with *tension and conflict* to further the *character's emotional development* and provide THEMATIC SIGNIFICANCE.

The thematic significance ties your entire story together. It is the reason you wrote your story, or what you hope to prove by writing your story.

If you are one of the lucky ones, you know the theme of your piece. You have already begun developing the thematic significance through the use of just the right details.

If the thematic significance of your story eludes you for now, keep track of themes that come to you as you write. In this way you can expand and exploit these themes when you discover the overall thematic significance of your story.

Chapter thirteen gives you techniques to explore thematic significance.

PLOT REDEFINED

Another way to view plot is to consider how the dramatic action changes or transforms the protagonist's character emotional development at depth, over time, in a thematically meaningful way. Like the first definition, this definition highlights the three primary plot threads—dramatic action, character emotional development, and thematic significance—that make up the three core dynamics of plot in every great story. This definition stresses an actual character change or transformation, while the first definition includes the all-important aspect of cause and effect.

OTHER LAYERS OF PLOT

Beyond the primary layers of plot we just reviewed, you can also plot out other aspects of your story: the setting, the history, the politics, the weather, the romance, and the mystery and suspense. However, in this book, we will only concern ourselves with the layers we just outlined; you are free to explore the others when you conceptualize your plot.

Relax. We are getting ahead of ourselves here. Breathe. Remember: The harder you try to get this, the harder it is for the information to penetrate your brain. Stand up. Shake out your hands. Stretch your neck by rotating your head slowly from side to side. Feel better? Let's proceed.

Chapter Two

HOW TO
USE THE
PLOT PLANNER

The Plot Planner is a visual plotting tool that many writers, myself included, find helpful in plotting fiction, memoirs, creative nonfiction, and screenplays. It serves as a great teaching tool for planning, pacing, keeping track of, testing, fixing, and refining a plot. Consider it a bridge between the invisible world of creativity and the visible world of the five senses.

Before you actually copy the Plot Planner onto a piece of banner paper, read through this chapter, which elaborates on the benefits of using the Plot Planner, the formats it appears in, and how it relates to both plot and character development. Chapter three will take you through the actual creation of your Plot Planner.

The best predictor for success is not talent alone. It is the amount of deliberate practice you are willing to commit to for your project's completion.

THE BENEFITS OF USING A PLOT PLANNER

A Plot Planner helps you visualize your story. Use it to do the following:

- Place your ideas and sequence your scenes to greatest effect.

- Experiment with changes in the storyline or presentation to evoke stronger reaction and interest from the reader.
- Get a sense of how your story is paced.
- Collaborate with others by showing them where you need help with your plot.
- Generate ideas to better develop your story.
- Solidify your understanding of the story's core elements.
- Ensure you understand the story you are presenting.

Most important, the Plot Planner enables you to keep the larger picture of your story in full view as you concentrate on writing individual scenes. It maintains paramount focus on crafting a story that conveys your core message to your reader and audience in a compelling and meaningful way.

FORMATS FOR THE PLOT PLANNER

The Plot Planner can be displayed in two different formats. In both formats, notice how the line moves steadily higher, building your story slowly and methodically as tension increases. Each scene delivers more tension and conflict than the preceding scene, with intensity building to your story's climax.

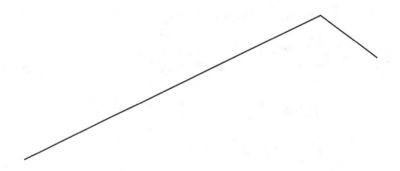

Format 1

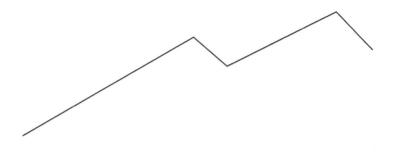

Format 2

When I started teaching plot intensives, I described the design of the Plot Planner as waves cresting. Typically the structure of a short story builds to one giant wave in which a crisis serves as the story's climax. (This mirrors Format 1.) Novels, memoirs, creative nonfiction, and screenplays have two peak moments: the dark night or crisis and the ultimate climactic moment.

In the second case, the crisis and the climax are written as separate scenes. (This is reflected in Format 2.) Again, there are no rules; use the format of the Plot Planner that best supports your story.

The flow of a story emanates from dramatic action, character emotional development, and thematic significance. The Chinese call this flow in humans *qi* (pronounced "chi"). The *qi* directs and coordinates the flow of energies and is the mainstay of one's life force. *Qi* cannot be touched or seen, but it is inherently present in all things.

Everything in the world is either energy or matter. You write your story on a computer, which is matter. You are composed of matter. Your story and your characters are not matter; they *are* pure energy, a magical series of events that occurs first in your imagination and then in the imaginations of your readers. A story is about things happening to people and the world around them, and is thus made up of energy. The energy of a story doesn't remain flat, just as the Plot

Planner line isn't flat. A story grows in intensity, which is reflected in the line moving steadily higher as the stakes and the energy of the story also rise.

Characters move and make things happen. Tension builds. Each scene shows more conflict than the one that came before. Each defeat the character suffers is more intense and more costly, and creates incrementally higher degrees of difficulty to overcome, as reflected in the direction of the Plot Planner line.

PLOTTING ABOVE AND BELOW THE LINES

A story depicts the shifting of power back and forth between the protagonist and the antagonists. Ultimately, story is about struggle on the way to character change and transformation.

In every great story, a protagonist pushes toward something (her goal), while forces both internal and external attempt to thwart her progress. This struggle between the protagonist and the antagonists sends the energy of your story soaring. The more powerful and formidable the antagonists, the greater the intensity, drama, and excitement in the scene.

Antagonists fall within one of six standard categories:

1. **ANOTHER CHARACTER:** family, friends, co-workers, enemies, lovers
2. **NATURE:** hurricanes, earthquakes, floods, natural law, physical disabilities
3. **SOCIETY:** religious institutions, government, customs, gangs
4. **MACHINE:** cars, robots, spaceships, motorcycles
5. **GOD:** spiritual beliefs
6. **PROTAGONIST:** inner life, past mistakes, fears, flaws, doubts, moral choices, willpower

The main struggle of the story is between the protagonist, who wants something enough to take action against all odds, and the antagonist(s) or forces within and without the protagonist who work against her.

As the character prepares to confront the adversity, suspense builds and the reader begins to participate. The character reacts after experiencing the opposition and helps build a bridge to her emotional state. Adversity doesn't have to be present in every scene; the scenes that come before and after the opposition are just as important.

How does this relate to the Plot Planner? At its core, the Plot Planner is merely a line that separates scenes filled with conflict and excitement (which appear above the Plot Planner line) from those that are passive, filled with summary and backstory, or heavy with information (which appear below the Plot Planner line). More important, the Plot Planner line divides scenes into those where the energy, power, or control is with the antagonist, forcing the protagonist to react (above the Plot Planner line) and those where the protagonist controls the direction of the action or holds the power over the antagonist (below the Plot Planner line).

By placing ideas above or below the Plot Planner line, you create a visual map for analyzing critical story information, presentation flow, and weaknesses in your story's overall sequence. You are also able to track how the energy of your story rises and falls.

Above the Line

Like the surface of the sea with its white caps and waves and swells, the external, gripping territory of the dramatic action, when your protagonist is out of control, fearful, lost, confused, or under the power of an antagonist, belongs above the line. All scenes that show complications, conflicts, tension, dilemmas, and suspense where the protagonist is forced away from her goals belong above the line.

In summary, scenes that show action where the power is somewhere other than with the protagonist go *above* the Plot Planner line. They can include the following:

- tension
- conflict
- suspense

- catastrophe
- the unknown
- betrayal
- being chased or pursued
- deception
- vengeance
- rebellion
- persecution
- rivalry
- conspiracy
- criminal action against the protagonist
- suspicion

Scenes that show character emotional development involving the following also belong *above* the Plot Planner line:

- loss
- failure to cope
- revenge
- self-sacrifice
- loss of control
- anger
- poor decision-making
- grief
- criminal action taken by the protagonist
- fear
- rebellion
- greed
- unhappiness
- personal flaw
- loss of power

Below the Line

Below the line is where the mystery lies. Scenes that belong below the line show the undertow: the internal, emotional territory of the protagonist. Much of the character emotional development is placed be-low the line, because character development often is revealed through character introspection. Any scenes that slow the energy of the story or in which the power shifts back to the protagonist belong below the line.

Scenes where the protagonist is proactive rather than reactive, or is deciding the best course of action to accomplish her goals and then taking it, belong below the Plot Planner line. These scenes can include the following:

- a lull in conflict, tension, and suspense
- a sharing of information with the reader by telling rather than showing

Scenes in which the protagonist is doing one of the following also belong *below* the Plot Planner line:

- remaining calm
- coping
- solving problems
- staying in control
- planning
- searching inward
- contemplating

THE STRUCTURE OF STORIES

Understanding the structure of a novel is paramount to using the Plot Planner to best effect. A story can usually be divided into three parts: the beginning, the middle, and the end. Remember, however, that rules are made to be broken.

Part One: The Beginning

Part One of the story begins on page 1. Part One is approximately 25 percent of your entire story. Part One usually ends with a turning point scene or cluster of scenes called the end of the beginning. Most writers find it easy to write seventy-five pages of compelling beginning scenes but struggle to keep the momentum going beyond the end of the beginning.

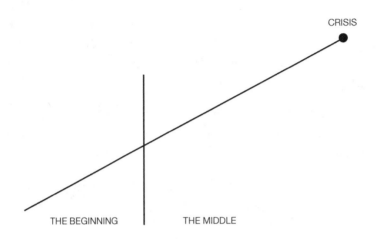

CRISIS

THE BEGINNING   THE MIDDLE

Part Two: The Middle

The middle is the longest portion of the story—approximately 50 percent of the total—and contains the most scenes. This is where many writers come up short. Daunted by the long expanse that awaits them, they stop in despair.

Part Two generally ends soon after the character reaches the false summit on her mountain journey, the crisis.

The Crisis

The crisis is where the energy of the story reaches its highest point so far, and it is where the tension and conflict peak. In facing the greatest fear, pain, or disappointment, or the most unexpected shock, betrayal, or failure, the protagonist is forced to see herself clearly for the first time. In some cultures, this time is referred to as the dark night of the soul. It is a major turning point. Will the protagonist ignore the wake-up call? Or will she grow and change as a result of the crisis?

As I mentioned earlier in this chapter, if you are writing a short story, the crisis may be the highest point of the piece. In short stories, generally speaking, there need be only one high point.

In a novel, once the protagonist has been hit with the crisis, the story is not over—the crisis is actually a false summit. Once she arrives as the crisis, however, the true summit becomes visible. The dip in Format 2 of the Plot Planner is where the energy of the story drops, giving the reader time to breathe after the excitement of the crisis and before the protagonist undertakes the journey to the climax.

Part Three: The End

The end of the story is comprised of the last 25 percent of the entire narrative.

The end is made up of three parts: the buildup to the climax, the climax itself, and the resolution.

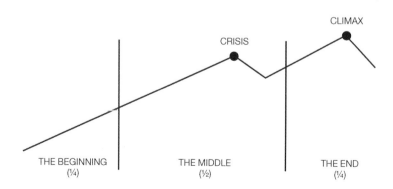

THE BEGINNING (¼)   THE MIDDLE (½)   THE END (¼)

The Buildup to the Climax

The protagonist enters the end of the story wiser, having suffered the setback at the crisis. The goal she sets for herself in the end determines the dramatic action in the scenes building up to the climax. That same goal also determines the antagonists she will meet as she moves forward. She is stronger and wiser now. So, too, are the antagonists determined to stand in her way.

The Climax

The energy of your story has been building scene by scene. Now, at the climax, it reaches a crescendo.

The climax is similar to the crisis in that it is another major turning point of high drama. But if the protagonist is given a chance to view herself clearly during the crisis, the climax is her opportunity to show if and how she has indeed grown, changed, learned, and transformed. After the crisis, the protagonist might say with full conviction that she will never be the same. But it is one thing to say it and quite another to actually do it. At our core, all of us have a natural tendency to resist change, preferring to hold tight to the comfort of the familiar. To stretch and grow and change involves the unknown. Rather than risk the possibility of failure, most of us would rather not even try. The climax involves some sort of action that forces the protagonist to show the reader who she is at her core now that she has experienced all she has throughout the story.

Old habits are tough to break. A character who has been put in a high-conflict, high-tension situation will first fall back into old ways. The suspense increases. The reader knows the protagonist has sworn she has changed. Will she act accordingly?

The Resolution

The resolution is where you tie up loose ends. Not all of the subplots need to be resolved by the end of the story, but the important ones do. Tie up only enough so that you provide thematic meaning to your overall project.

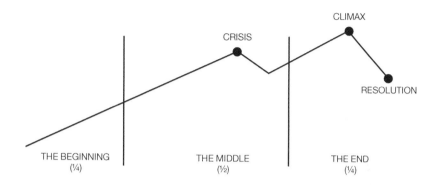

CLIMAX

CRISIS

RESOLUTION

THE BEGINNING
(¼)

THE MIDDLE
(½)

THE END
(¼)

TIPS FOR CREATING PLOT

- Plot is as much about pacing as it is about the dramatic action and the transformation the character undergoes. To satisfy your readers, placement and pacing of each scene becomes critical.
- If you spend too many words or pages in the beginning of the piece, it increases your chances of losing your reader right off the bat. Readers want to be grounded in the story, they want to understand who is who and what is what in the story, and then they want something big to happen.
- The balance between backstory and front story, between internal dialogue and overt action, and between character development and action is delicate and must always be kept in mind.
- Just because you write your story in a certain order does not mean that is where the scene or summary or narration will stay.
- Placement and pacing are under your control, are essential to plot, and are best seen and understood against the backdrop of a Plot Planner.

THE BEGINNING
(¼)

Candle in the Window by Christina Dodd

This Plot Planner uses symbols to indicate scenes that show the character emotional development of Lady Saura of Roget (Δ) and Sir William of Miravel (□), as well as the dramatic action (∞) and thematic significance (✓).

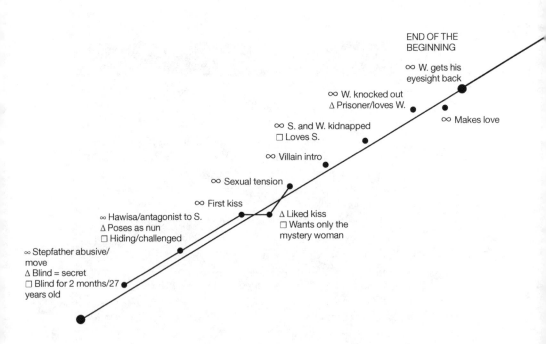

END OF THE BEGINNING

∞ W. gets his eyesight back

∞ W. knocked out
Δ Prisoner/loves W.

∞ Makes love

∞ S. and W. kidnapped
□ Loves S.

∞ Villain intro

∞ Sexual tension

∞ First kiss

∞ Hawisa/antagonist to S.
Δ Poses as nun
□ Hiding/challenged

Δ Liked kiss
□ Wants only the mystery woman

∞ Stepfather abusive/ move
Δ Blind = secret
□ Blind for 2 months/27 years old

THE MIDDLE
(½)

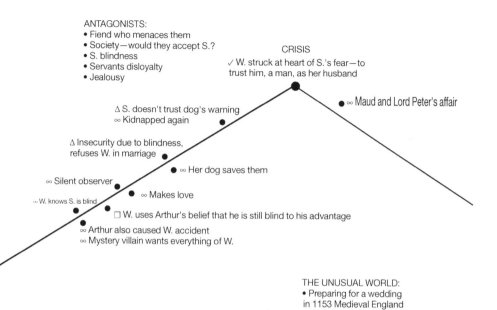

ANTAGONISTS:
- Fiend who menaces them
- Society—would they accept S.?
- S. blindness
- Servants disloyalty
- Jealousy

CRISIS
✓ W. struck at heart of S.'s fear—to trust him, a man, as her husband

● ∞ Maud and Lord Peter's affair

Δ S. doesn't trust dog's warning
∞ Kidnapped again ●

Δ Insecurity due to blindness, refuses W. in marriage ●

● ∞ Her dog saves them

∞ Silent observer ●

● ∞ Makes love

∾ W. knows S. is blind

□ W. uses Arthur's belief that he is still blind to his advantage

∞ Arthur also caused W. accident
∞ Mystery villain wants everything of W.

THE UNUSUAL WORLD:
- Preparing for a wedding in 1153 Medieval England

KEY
Δ Character Emotional Development for Lady Saura of Roget
□ Character Emotional Development for Sir William of Miravel
∞ Dramatic Action
✓ Thematic Significance

Download a larger version of this Plot Planner at
www.writersdigest.com/writing-blockbuster-plots.

THE END
(¼)

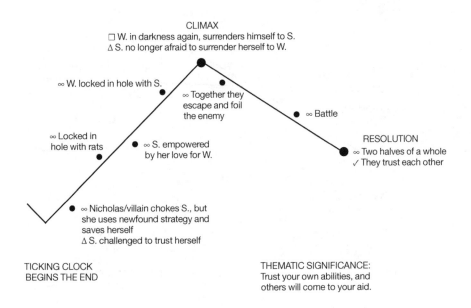

CLIMAX
☐ W. in darkness again, surrenders himself to S.
Δ S. no longer afraid to surrender herself to W.

∞ W. locked in hole with S.

∞ Together they
escape and foil
the enemy

∞ Battle

∞ Locked in
hole with rats

∞ S. empowered
by her love for W.

RESOLUTION
∞ Two halves of a whole
✓ They trust each other

∞ Nicholas/villain chokes S., but
she uses newfound strategy and
saves herself
Δ S. challenged to trust herself

TICKING CLOCK
BEGINS THE END

THEMATIC SIGNIFICANCE:
Trust your own abilities, and
others will come to your aid.

KEY
Δ Character Emotional Development for Lady Saura of Roget
☐ Character Emotional Development for Sir William of Miravel
∞ Dramatic Action
✓ Thematic Significance

Download a larger version of this Plot Planner at
www.writersdigest.com/writing-blockbuster-plots.

Chapter Three

PLOT PLANNER PARAMETERS

The Plot Planner is divided into Part One: The Beginning, Part Two: The Middle, and Part Three: The End. Before you construct a Plot Planner for your project, it is best if you are able to determine the parameters of each part. In this chapter, I cover two ways to define those parameters.

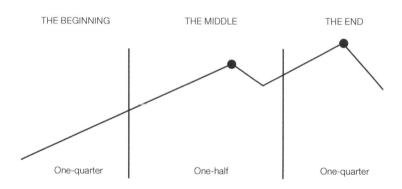

THE BEGINNING   THE MIDDLE   THE END

One-quarter   One-half   One-quarter

This entire chapter is optional. If you benefit from fixed, concrete guidelines for determining the breakdown of which scenes belong in the beginning, the middle, and the end of your plotline, read on. If you'd rather let your intuition decide, move to chapter four.

PLAN BY SCENE

Count the number of scenes you have written. Do you envision more or fewer upon completion? If you have not yet started a project, choose any number of scenes based on the scene count of successful novels in your genre and how you envision your story. Write down the total number of scenes.

_____ total scenes

Now divide the total number of scenes of your book by four to determine the number that should be devoted to each of the three parts of your book. (If there are only three parts, you might ask why you are dividing by four. I will explain the logic behind this in a moment.)

An average novel sold in bookstores typically consists of sixty scenes.

Part One: The Beginning Scenes

The beginning portion of your Plot Planner encompasses approximately one-quarter of the total scenes. Thus, if you have sixty scenes, the beginning portion has fifteen scenes. How many scenes are in the beginning portion of your project?

_____ beginning scenes

Part Two: The Middle Scenes

The middle portion of your Plot Planner encompasses approximately one-half of the total scenes. (This is why you divide by four—the middle is twice as long as either the beginning or the end.) If you have sixty scenes, the middle portion has thirty scenes. How many scenes are in the middle portion of your project?

_____ middle scenes

Part Three: The End Scenes

The end portion of your Plot Planner encompasses approximately one-quarter of the total scenes. If you have sixty scenes, the end portion contains the final fifteen scenes. How many scenes do you envision your story having in the end portion?

_____ end scenes

There is another way to determine the parameters of your plotline that is based on the number of pages in your book. If the numbers you generated in this first section fall into the approximate range, move on to chapter four. If analyzing the page count to determine the parameters better suits you than doing so based on scene count, keep reading.

PLAN BY PAGE COUNT

From an informal survey by *Publishers Weekly*, an insider's magazine on the publishing business, the average length of a novel is about 250 to 300 pages. That average length translates to between 60,000 and 90,000 words. Of course, there are exceptions, typically based on genre. A historical novel or a science fiction saga can run 500 pages or more. Keep in mind that the longer the book, the more expensive it is to produce, either for the publisher or for you, if you choose to self-publish. Either way, your readers end up paying those higher costs.

If you have finished a rough draft, determining the length of your book should be simple. If you have just started a project, estimate the length you envision for the final product based on books similar to yours that you admire.

_____ total pages

Now, use the same process you did in the scenes method. Divide the total number of pages of your book by four to determine the number of pages for each of the three parts.

Part One: The Beginning Page Count

The beginning portion of your Plot Planner will encompass approximately one-quarter of the total page count. If, for example, your novel is 300 pages total, the beginning portion equals 75 pages. How many pages do you envision your story's beginning?

_____ beginning pages

Part Two: The Middle Page Count

The middle portion of your Plot Planner will take up approximately one-half of the total page count of your project. If your novel is 300 pages total, the middle portion of the Plot Planner equals 150 pages. How many pages do you envision in the middle portion of your project?

_____ middle pages

Part Three: The End Page Count

The end portion of your Plot Planner will encompass approximately one-quarter of the total page count. If your novel is 300 pages total, the end portion equals 75 pages. How many pages do you envision in the end portion?

_____ end pages

With all of these numbers, you have a good sense of where the beginning of your story begins and ends, where the middle—the longest part of your project—begins and ends, and where the end begins and ends.

TAKE A BREAK

You didn't expect to do math to plot out your project, did you? This is it, I promise. You will use the numbers you generated here in the actual construction of your Plot Planner, but after that, no more numbers! And remember that these numbers are simply guidelines.

Before we move to the actual construction of your Plot Planner, why not sit back and look over your numbers. See your story in your mind. Take a deep breath. Invite in a spirit of discovery.

Chapter Four

CONSTRUCT YOUR PLOT PLANNER

To start, retrieve the numbers you generated in chapter three, as well as a roll of banner paper.

Adapt the following ideas in this chapter to stimulate a feeling of excitement, expectancy, and enthusiasm for your story. The looser you stay, the easier it is for discovery to flow. Confidence and joy create a safe atmosphere in which to explore. If, at any point, you are motivated to write, put your plotting work aside and do so.

As we discussed in the previous chapter, the Plot Planner is divided into three parts: Part One: The Beginning, Part Two: The Middle, and Part Three: The End. We will begin at the beginning.

There is no right or wrong to what I'm offering here. These are some ideas that have helped other writers, and I offer them to you so you do not have to go it alone. At the heart of this book lies the intention to support you in your writing.

THE BEGINNING

The beginning portion of your book ends with a scene of high intensity and meaning.

The beginning serves several functions:

- It establishes your contract with your readers by letting them know what your story is and is not about.
- It introduces the story's time and setting.
- It sets up the dramatic action and the underlying conflict.
- It introduces the protagonist and all the other major characters with an idea of who they are, their emotional makeup, and the weight they carry in the story.
- It introduces the protagonist's short-term goal and at least hints at a long-term goal.
- It introduces the theme of the overall project.

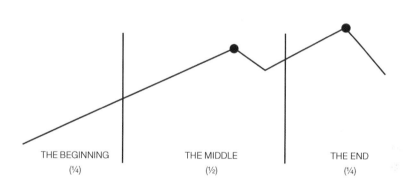

Now it is time to decide on the structure of the beginning portion of your project. Refer to the figures you generated in chapter three, or use your own judgment. A scene may stand out in your imagination because of its high dramatic action or because it shows the character's emotional development at its peak. If this scene also evokes a sense of leaving something behind—the character's innocence, restrictions, limitations, safety, or known world—for the unknown, use that scene to end the beginning portion of your Plot Planner.

As I've mentioned before, the parameters we set in chapter three are meant only as guidelines. It is not necessary to follow the figures exactly. For now, decide where you believe the beginning portion of your story begins and ends

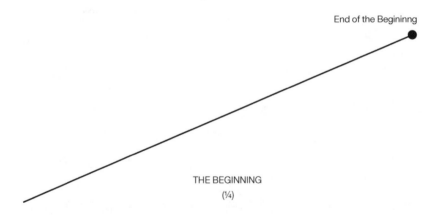 CREATE THE PLOT PLANNER

Position the banner paper so it lies horizontally on the table in front of you. Unroll only part of the paper, just a couple of feet, for now. Draw a line, starting about one-quarter of the height of the paper, so that it sweeps steadily upward. A fast-paced, high-action story demands a sharper and steeper line than does a slower, internal story, because it represents a sharper and steeper degree of intensity in the energy of the story as the beginning progresses.

End of the Begininng

THE BEGINNING
(¼)

At the end of the line, write "the end of the beginning" to mark where the beginning leaves off and the middle begins. Above the line, indicate how many scenes you envision for the first quarter of your story. Use the number for the beginning that you generated in chapter three.

THE END OF THE BEGINNING

The first peak in the Plot Planner represents the end of the beginning and generally occurs one-quarter of the way through the page or scene count.

To produce a powerful end of the beginning (and, for that matter, a powerful climax toward the end of the end), a writer must introduce everything in the beginning that will have an impact on the end of the beginning. Toward the end of the beginning, one door after another slams shut on the protagonist. For each of the closed and locked doors to bear significance, the reader must first have seen what is behind each door and understand what each one means to the character.

The beginning ends when the last door shuts and the character knows there is no turning back. The end of the beginning is a major turning point, the termination of everything the character knows. At this point, the protagonist has no choice but to go forward and face the unknown.

The end of the beginning is the first high point in the story, and it reflects the catalyst that propels the protagonist into the rest of the story. It marks an emotional peak for the protagonist. The incident or revelation or conflict that indicates the end of the beginning sets the true drama in motion.

The Pulitzer Prize–winning novel *All the Light We Cannot See* by Anthony Doerr contains two ends of the beginning: one for each of the protagonists. These ends of the beginning appear in alternating chapters. First comes a scene with Werner, an orphan in a mining town in Germany, on the day before his departure as he attempts to convince his younger sister that he will return from the school for "the best boys in Germany." She's old enough to understand the "atrocities" boys from this school are committing and refuses to accept his lies. "Ten hours later, he's on a train" bound for the school.

When the Nazis occupy Paris, Marie-Laure, a blind girl of twelve, flees Paris with her father to the walled citadel of Saint-Malo and her reclusive great-uncle. She leaves behind all she knows and enters the great unknown with her father and thousands of others. The unknown turns even more exotic as she takes up residence in a tall house by the sea. However, the true end of the beginning is in the chapter following Werner's end of the beginning scene when Marie-Laure finally meets her great-uncle, a character pivotal to both protagonist's plots.

CHANGING POV

If your story shifts the point of view between two or more main characters in alternating chapters, draw more than one Plot Planner line. Represent each shifting point of view, or any main characters who change and transform due to the dramatic action of the story, with a different Plot Planner line on your banner paper, one above the other, one line each for the two major characters. Use these lines to plot out the characters' individual plots. Develop a plot profile (see chapter eleven) for each character to help you envision their individual character transformations. This way you're sure to have two (or more) deeply developed characters, and you will be able to plot out their individual stories and how the two intertwine and reinforce the overall meaning of the story.

There. That's all there is to creating a Plot Planner for the beginning of your story.

The Plot Planner provides enough form and structure to tame chaos and bring meaning to all the ideas rolling around a writer's head.

Folly by Laurie R. King

This Plot Planner uses symbols to indicate scenes that show character emotional development (≈) and dramatic action (◊).

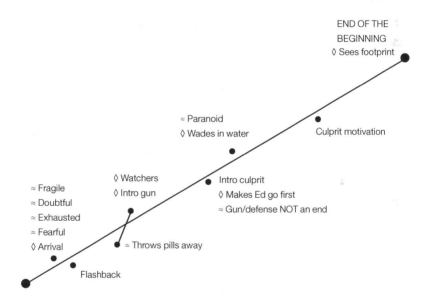

END OF THE
BEGINNING
◊ Sees footprint

≈ Paranoid
◊ Wades in water

Culprit motivation

◊ Watchers
◊ Intro gun

Intro culprit
◊ Makes Ed go first
≈ Gun/defense NOT an end

≈ Fragile
≈ Doubtful
≈ Exhausted
≈ Fearful
◊ Arrival

≈ Throws pills away

Flashback

KEY
≈ Character Emotional Development
◊ Dramatic Action

Chapter Five

PLOT
THE
BEGINNING

When plotting the beginning of your story, you will need to determine which scenes fall above and below the Plot Planner line. Determining whether the protagonist or antagonist(s) is in control in a given scene helps you decide where each scene belongs on the Plot Planner.

As we discussed earlier, scenes in which the dramatic action shows an antagonist controlling or holding the power over the protagonist go above the line. For instance, if the first scene shows the protagonist prevented from doing something she desires because of her insecurity, then the antagonist (her own flaw) is in charge, and that scene goes *above the line*.

Conversely, scenes in which the protagonist is in control belong below the line. These scenes are necessary to introduce the strengths and loves and dreams in her emotional development at the beginning of the story. If, in the first scene, the protagonist is in charge of the situation, or is at least not particularly threatened in any way, then scene one goes *below the line*.

Below-the-line scenes also give the reader a chance to take a breath after a particularly demanding dramatic action scene. But at their core, these scenes lack power and vitality. If you have too many of them in a row, you will put your reader to sleep.

> Begin the story above the line with some sort of tension or an unanswered question, and your reader will immediately be drawn into the story.

EXAMPLE

Before you dive in and begin plotting your beginning, let's take a look at how this works in action. In *Where the Heart Is* by Billie Letts, Novalee, the protagonist, is seventeen years old, seven months pregnant, and superstitious about the number seven. In the first few scenes, the antagonist is her boyfriend, Willy Jack.

The book opens in scene with Novalee and her boyfriend on their way from Oklahoma to California. Novalee needs to stop to use the bathroom, but they have already stopped once for the same reason, and Novalee knows it is too soon to ask again. Tension mounts as her bladder causes her more and more discomfort and, eventually, pain.

Because this scene is rife with tension, and because Willy Jack holds the power, rather than Novalee, scene one goes above the line on the Plot Planner.

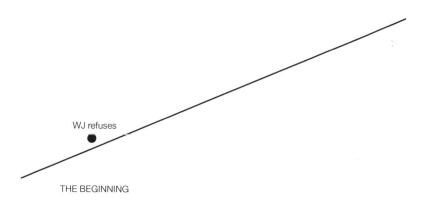

WJ refuses

THE BEGINNING

In the next scene, Novalee awakens from a dream to find that her shoes fell through the rusted-out hole in the floorboard of the car. Willy Jack agrees to stop at a Wal-Mart to replace the shoes. After Novalee uses the bathroom, she buys some rubber thongs and receives $7.77 in change. She runs outside and discovers that the car and Willy Jack are gone.

This scene, scene two, also goes above the line, because although Novalee starts the scene in control of the situation, the scene ends in disaster.

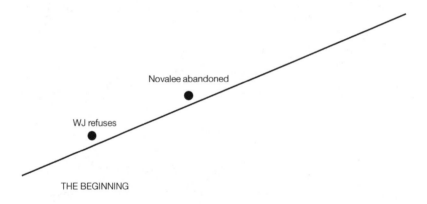

Novalee abandoned

WJ refuses

THE BEGINNING

In the next several scenes, Novalee meets three people, each of whom will play a part in her life as the story progresses, though readers do not know this at the time. Characters are best introduced in the beginning in order of their importance to the story. In this story, these three characters quickly become pivotal to her plot.

Not much happens in these scenes. This is a risky way to go about the start of a story; we are only on page 17. Usually the writer keeps things moving in the beginning of a project to entice the reader into the dreamscape of the story. However, in this case, slowing down works because there is so much tension hovering over the story.

The fact that Novalee is pregnant, in the middle of nowhere, and has only $7.77 adds suspense to the broader dramatic question (Will she or won't she succeed?) to carry these quieter scenes.

The reader flips the pages to learn how this young girl is going to take care of herself. Each time Novalee meets someone, the reader waits for her to ask for help, and each time Novalee keeps quiet, the tension builds ever higher.

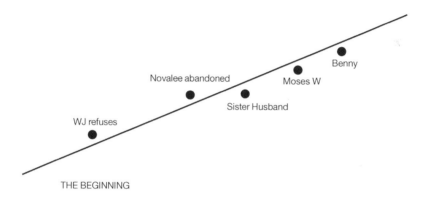

The presence of a "looming unknown" makes it possible for you to slow things down without the fear of losing your readers.

✏️ PLOT THE BEGINNING

With your Plot Planner in front of you, decide which of your scenes, either already written or simply imagined, go above the line and which ones go below it. If your first scene has tension and conflict, or if the power is with someone or something other than the protagonist, jot a short note for this scene above the line on the Plot Planner, e.g., "Novalee abandoned." Sticky notes work well for this task because they come in different colors and shapes, which you can use for identifying different plotlines, and they allow you to move and rearrange scenes quickly and easily.

If there is no tension or conflict in scene one, then the scene sticky note belongs below the line.

Now move to the next scene. Does scene two go above or below the line? Write it in. Continue in this way. Stop when you've written your scenes or scene ideas for the turning point of your story, the end of the beginning. Once you are finished with the scenes in the beginning portion of your book, stop and take a look at how they are arranged on the Plot Planner.

If most of your scenes are above the line, you can be confident that there is enough dramatic action to keep your reader turning the pages to find out what happens next. If, however, you find that most of your scenes are below the line, you could be in trouble. There is no rule for how many scenes belong above or below the line; however, if too many scenes in a row are below the line, it could mean that your story is too passive, too flat, and contains too much telling. Your story may not contain enough excitement for the reader, nor enough tension or conflict.

Many scenes that belong below the line are filled with internal monologue and, thus, are inherently nondramatic, with little action. Internal conflict is essentially nondramatic in that it cannot be played out moment by moment on the page. Do not get me wrong—internal conflict is essential for depth. But external dramatic action shows the degree of conflict and makes the scene. Scene, in turn, makes the story.

Tension in the Beginning

If you are like most writers, you probably find that the beginning scenes are the easiest to generate. As you plot beginning scenes on the Plot Planner, you might be pleased to find that the tension rises and that these scenes reveal a nice flow in cause and effect.

You should note that the line of the Plot Planner is not flat but climbs steadily higher. This corresponds with the rising tension of your beginning scenes. Much more is at stake in scene ten than in scene one.

As you plot the beginning, make sure your protagonist is an active participant in her own story. Novalee is a sympathetic character because she is, at her core, a good person attempting to do the right thing. She is also a survivor. This is important—the protagonist of a story cannot be passive. As the tension and conflict continue to rise, the protagonist must demonstrate that she can pick herself up off the floor time and time again. No matter how bad things get, find a way to make them even worse—and make sure your protagonist rises to each challenge.

If the protagonist is in worse shape at the end of a scene than at the beginning, you—as the writer—are in good shape. The emotion of the scene is constantly changing and the tension remains high.

Sharing Information and Backstory with the Reader

Writers, especially beginning writers, often are tempted to blurt out everything up front. This results in flashbacks popping up early on in the story in order to reveal the character's backstory or the event that first sent the protagonist off-kilter.

My advice: In the beginning, pace how much information you share with the reader and refrain from using flashbacks. Short memories are fine, but try not to move back and forth in time. Rather your main objective for now is to ground the reader in the here and now of the story, where the main action takes place. In each scene, especially in the beginning, put in only as much information as is needed to inform that particular scene. (This can include foreshadowing clues of what is to come, but don't overload the scenes with such details.) Invite the reader in slowly but with a bang. Keep curiosity high to create a page-turner!

The first quarter of any writing project introduces the story's major characters, their goals, the setting, time period, themes, and issues. This is not the place where you necessarily deepen the character or the plot; it is the place of introduction.

When I say to introduce the familiar—such as characters, habits, the setting, or the character's thought patterns—do not confuse introduction with passivity. Draw in the reader with dramatic action that calls for conflict, tension, suspense, and/or curiosity.

Once you have plotted out your beginning scenes, re-evaluate the end of the beginning scene you determined in chapter four. You want a scene(s) that cause substantial experiences:

- a separation from life as she has always known it
- a shift in her life circumstances or belief system
- a fracture in her primary relationship(s) (with others and even with herself)

Plot the effect as the protagonist leaves everything behind at the end of this beginning portion of your Plot Planner line. At the end of the beginning, there is no turning back. The protagonist crosses into the middle.

KEEP WRITING

If the activity above stimulates ideas and answers for your story, go back to the actual writing. Even when you lack the energy for writing, continue to show up each day. Instead of turning on your computer, turn to your Plot Planner.

My intention is to expose you to guidelines that work so that when you break the rules, you do so deliberately to achieve a specific result.

PLOT BY
CAUSE AND EFFECT

Congratulations! You have begun the process of plotting out your story. Before you test your scenes for cause and effect, take a few minutes to examine the beginning portion of your Plot Planner.

How many scenes were you able to plot above the line? How many scenes are arranged below the line? Were you honest about the scenes you put above the line? Do they indeed have some sort of tension and conflict? Does the power reside with someone or something other than the protagonist? Yes? Terrific! Still not sure? That's okay. As long as you can justify why you put them where you did, that is sufficient for now.

Perhaps you have only a few sticky notes strung along the beginning portion of your Plot Planner line. Your imagination has stalled, and you're struggling to come up with scene ideas to fill in all the looming blank spaces. If this is the case, you can generate scene ideas that produce unexpected twists and turns in your story by utilizing the concept of cause and effect.

USING CAUSE AND EFFECT

Plot is a series of scenes that are deliberately arranged by cause and effect *...*

What does that mean? Cause and effect are critical elements to plotting out your novels, short stories, memoirs, and creative nonfiction.

If you utilize cause and effect as you plot, you ensure that the events that happen in one scene cause the events that happen in the next scene. If you are able to link your scenes by cause and effect, each scene is organic. From the seeds you plant in the first scene grow the fruits of the next scene.

A story is made up of scenes with a clear dependence on each other. The conflict at the center of a scene represents the motivating cause that sets a series of events in motion. As you test your scenes for cause and effect, notice how some features of your story are more important than others. Look for patterns, and see which elements lead to the thematic significance of your story and which do not.

Cause and effect within and between scenes allows you to seamlessly lead the reader to each major turning point by linking the cause in one scene to the effect in the next scene. This sequencing allows the energy of the story to rise smoothly.

AVOIDING EPISODIC SCENES

Let me give you an example of what is *not* cause and effect. Say you are looking at the arrangement of the scenes in your story. Do you find yourself saying, "This event happens first, and then this happens next, and then this happens next, and then …"? You get the picture. If you ever hear an agent or editor tell you that your story is "too episodic" or "not causally linked," he or she means that your scenes are not strongly linked by cause and effect.

Scenes are episodic if they are not linked by cause and effect. If scenes are linked by cause and effect, each scene is meaningful to all the other scenes. Episodic events and random incidents are either boring or disconcerting.

Keep in mind that for every story where the causality sequence breaks down, where scenes come out of the blue, or where the story turns episodic and fails to connect with the reader, there are also those stories that shine with a looser, less-causally related arrangement. The presentation of most of the key scenes of *All the Light We Cannot See* could be labeled as episodic. Ultimately all of the scenes in the novel do tie together masterfully; however, by deciding not to link his scenes tightly together from one scene to the next, and by changing point-of-view characters and switching from one time period to another and then back, Doerr may cause readers some initial confusion and disorientation. Yet by using suspense at the end of each transitional scene and leaving the reader dangling from the cliff of not knowing what's coming, he speeds the story from one nonlinear event to the next.

If you're able to connect key scenes by cause and effect, either directly by linking one scene to the next or indirectly by twisting time, you will not be told your work is episodic. Instead the reader will be able to disappear seamlessly and effortlessly into the story.

Cause and effect is helpful in tying scenes together. It can also deepen the character's emotional development by conveying the effect of external events, people, and places on her emotions. For example, in one scene, a character responds emotionally to an event that interferes with her reaching her goal, like her mother's death, a bad breakup, an embezzlement, or a betrayal. In the next scene, we see the outcome of that emotional response, which, in turn, becomes the cause for another emotional effect.

To test if your story is tight and if your scenes are arranged by cause and effect, see if you can go from scene to scene and say, "In this scene, this event happens. *Because* that happens, then this happens, and *because* that happens, then this next conflict arises."

Do you notice the rhythm? What you planted in the first scene emerges in the next scene. The second scene cannot happen without the first scene happening. The third scene happens *because* the first two scenes unfolded before it. Each element is linked.

We are always striving to find meaning in the bigger picture, both in our own lives and in the stories we write. We want to know why one event gives rise to the next—to feel the inevitability of cause and effect. Your readers will expect that the events that unfold in one scene will have repercussions in the next.

LINKING SCENES THROUGH CHOSEN DETAILS

When you find a scene in your story that does not arise from the scene that comes before it, see if you can introduce an element, perhaps in a sentence or two, designed to lead into the next scene without shifting the focus of the current scene. For instance, say that the theme of the story is "The answers are always right in front of you." If scene one ends with the protagonist staring into a telescope, scene two could start with the protagonist dusting or moving the telescope. Adding details like this is not as satisfying as incorporating true cause and effect, but it at least provides a sense of continuity in nonrelated scenes.

If you find that even this strategy of linking scenes through chosen details does not work for you, then you may need to cut that scene or tweak it in such a way that it becomes the effect of the scene that comes before it or is at least connected to all the other scenes in the bigger story. You cannot stick a scene in your story just because the writing is beautiful or the format intriguing. You owe it to the reader to provide meaning.

Think of conflict in scene as the cause. The character's reaction to that cause is the effect the conflict has on the character. When the character responds to the conflict, his actions create yet another cause and, in turn, another effect. The story then moves from scene to scene by cause and effect. Every part plays into the whole, and the result is a satisfying story.

EXAMPLE

If we go from scene to scene in *Where the Heart Is* by Billie Letts, we discover well-established and carefully placed cause and effect. *Because* Novalee is pregnant, she frequently has to ask Willy Jack to stop the car so she can use the bathroom. Because Willy Jack refuses to stop, Novalee is forced to ask him, yet again, to stop. *Because*

Novalee keeps asking Willy Jack to stop, he abandons her. *Because* he abandons her, Novalee meets three crucial characters: Sister Husband, Moses W., and Benny.

Because each scene is linked to the one that came before it and the one that comes after, we draw a line from one to the next on the Plot Planner to indicate that the connection is unbroken.

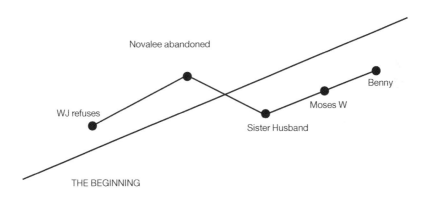

PLOTTING NONLINEAR STORIES

You may chose to organize the scenes of your story in a nonlinear progression, meaning that rather than present your scenes in chronological order from beginning to end in a straight line, you arrange them out of order. *The Time Traveler's Wife* by Audrey Niffenegger and *All the Light We Cannot See* are brilliantly portrayed out of chronological order and without following a tight causality pattern.

Linking scenes by tight cause and effect proves difficult, if not downright impossible, in a story where scenes are arranged and presented out of their natural order of occurrence. To help readers navigate through her story, Niffenegger presents the scenes of her two main characters, husband and wife Henry and Claire, using different strategies. Claire always moves through her scenes chronologically, as this is how she experiences time. However, Henry has the ability to time travel. His scenes reflect his time traveling as he hurls into the past, is yanked back to real time, and is spun into the future. The challenge in presenting the story out of order both in time and in cause and effect is to smooth the way so the reader doesn't become confused. Until readers are familiar and comfortable with the way the story is presented, the beginning scenes of *The Time Traveler's Wife* can be difficult to follow.

Rather than reporting a straight chain of events influenced by cause and effect and dependent on a sequential development of scenes, *All the Light We Cannot See* presents a time line that skips around. In the World War II love story, Marie-Laure and Werner grow up in the shadow of war and then attempt to survive the ensuing devastation. This story portrays the events of their lives by moving back and forth in time before, during, and after the invasion. However, the nonlinear structure is a benefit, not a detriment, to the story; it creates added depth that a more linear cause-and-effect presentation would have lacked.

In a nonlinear story, ensure your scenes move seamlessly and remain thematically true, even without the help of tight cause and effect. Before writing your scenes out of order, first plot them out on a Plot Planner in chronological order. This allows you to better manipulate the scenes and create the greatest dramatic action, excitement, meaning, and character emotional development when you later mix up the time sequence.

▭▶ PLOT THE CAUSE AND EFFECT IN THE BEGINNING

It's time to test whether the scenes you plotted from the beginning of your story are arranged by cause and effect.

Start at scene one. Say to yourself, "In scene one, this event happens." Now ask yourself, "Does what happens in scene one cause scene two?" If so, draw a line linking scene one to scene two. If not, leave a blank space between these scenes on the Plot Planner.

Now move to scene two. Again, ask yourself if what happens in scene two causes the conflict or action in scene three.

Move from scene to scene, asking yourself if one scene causes another. Each time you find cause and effect taking place, draw a line from one scene to the next to indicate the linkage between the two. Continue in this way until you arrive at the end of the beginning.

Do not worry if every scene is not influenced by cause and effect. As with the other techniques in this book, the discussion in this chapter is just a guideline. A working knowledge of cause and effect helps to ensure that you are building a satisfying story structure. The more adept you are at creating cause and effect, the better.

If you find that, in most cases, the story flows naturally from one scene to the next through cause and effect, you are in good shape. However, if you find that the story is episodic, then you will benefit from further exploration into the aspects of cause and effect.

Viewing your story as a whole on your Plot Planner and determining the causality between scenes and the overall coherence of your story gives insight into how you can turn all your scenes into the driving force behind an exceptional story.

Without cause and effect, the tempo and intensity of the story can bog down, and the writer can get stuck.

Chapter Seven

PLOT
THE
MIDDLE

The middle of your book comprises approximately one-half of all of the scenes in your entire project. It is where the main action of your story takes place. Perhaps you left the beginning on a high note and launched enthusiastically toward the middle. You and your characters have now crossed into the heart of the story world. However, if you're unprepared and don't know how to proceed, the middle can seem like a long, empty expanse, like a huge wasteland waiting to devour you, the writer. The middle has stopped many good writers in their tracks.

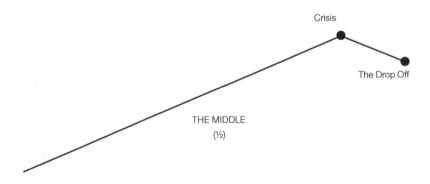

Crisis

The Drop Off

THE MIDDLE
(½)

> The middle is especially difficult for writers because it requires them to create continually rising tension.

Writing the middle of a novel, memoir, or screenplay has a bad reputation. Granted it's easy to get lost in the maze of subplots and secondary characters that populate the middle. Creating twists and turns in this portion of the story can make you dizzy. In your confusion, doubt can creep in, and you might question why you ever decided to take on such a project. The crisis awaits, and the thought of ripping the rug out from under the character you've grown to love makes you weep.

If you are like other writers, at this point you are desperate to return to the place of discovery. To ease your way out of the terror of the unknown, you might retreat to the beginning of the story and start again. You rationalize that just as soon as you incorporate all those loose ends, you will be better prepared to persevere to the End. Yet, inevitably, when you arrive at the point in the middle where you stopped before, you flounder yet again.

Sound familiar? Rather than rip the Plot Planner off the wall and stuff it in the bottom of your filing cabinet, I encourage you to keep at it. You probably believe that your story suffers a fatal flaw. That is not necessarily so.

I bring up the difficulty of the middle not to frighten you but to prepare you. After all, your attitude directly affects your energy as you write, which, in turn, affects the energy of your project. The last thing I want is to send your energy spiraling downward. Understand that when you hit a brick wall, it is not because of you. It is the nature of the beast.

To avoid hitting that wall, keep in mind the five primary goals of the middle. Look for opportunities in every scene in the middle of your novel, memoir, or screenplay to do the following:

1. Deepen the protagonist's character traits, both positive and negative, that you introduced in the beginning.
2. Create an unfamiliar world that keeps her off balance.

3. Develop secondary characters with goals at odds and in conflict with the protagonist's goals.

4. Intensify the uncertainty of the outcome and the dramatic question ("Will she or won't she succeed?") by intensifying the demands of her opposition.

5. Show her learning new skills and being exposed to new beliefs that she'll need to succeed in the End. She might not even consciously or fully understand how the skills will serve her in the future. These lessons and tricks should be part of the external plot of the middle and directly relate to one or more of the secondary characters as part of their shared subplots. The talents, powers, and moves obtained or taken by the protagonist should play into the plot in the final quarter of the story, but neither the characters nor the reader should know of their importance in the middle.

Following these guidelines for the middle of your story will help you show up, day after day, to write. You can devise some bumps and challenges that will interfere with the protagonist's progress. Your page count might double as you expose your protagonist to new skills and talents that she'll need for the End. You'll begin to feel confident and excited.

A writer in one of my workshops once asked a fellow writer to stand up and hold out his arm sideways with his thumb pointing down. Then she instructed him to resist when she pressed down on his arm. He was able to keep his arm steady against the pressure.

Next, she asked him to think about something negative concerning his writing. This time, using the same pressure, his arm gave way, as if he had lost all of his strength.

Finally she asked him to concentrate on a positive experience or feeling. He was easily able to resist the pressure on his arm.

This experiment shows how negative emotions, like worry and doubt and criticism, affect our physical energy. It also illustrates the strengthening effect that positive thoughts and emotions have on us physically.

I encourage you to stay positive as you tackle the exotic world of the middle. Take a look at all of the scenes you have plotted out on the Plot Planner. Do not see the Plot Planner as half empty; see it as half full. The direction of your focus does not change the reality of the holes and gaps that are on your Plot Planner, but your attitude certainly changes your energy and enthusiasm to persevere.

Determination and perseverance are two key traits of successful writers. Stay determined. Persevere all the way to the end of your project. Until you reach the end, you will never truly know what you have.

THE ANATOMY OF THE MIDDLE

The middle is where the real trouble for the protagonist begins. It must inject in the reader a strong desire to know what happens next. Sometimes the tension level in the middle starts at a lower place on the Plot Planner line than at the end of the beginning. This happens when the tension of the beginning drops slightly, having found a release by moving into the unfamiliar world of the middle. Also, the middle doesn't always pick up where the end of the beginning left off. By beginning the middle with a time jump or a new location, a writer makes the end of the beginning even more definite.

Often, as a result of what happens at the end of the beginning, the protagonist enters the middle with a radically different goal than she started with in the story. The more specific these two goals are—the goal that informs the beginning and the goal she obtains from the middle onward—the better. These goals become plot beacons, and the protagonist carefully makes her way toward the blinking lights. Both goals are always just out of reach, thanks to obstacles that lead the character off track.

The middle is often known as the land of the antagonists. As we've discussed, antagonists are great tools for keeping the action high and increasing both tension and conflict. The protagonist encounters one antagonist after another, and conflicts and obstacles prevent her from reaching her long-term goal. Whether internal or external, when antagonists are in control, the protagonist is out of control, and, thus, the line on your Plot Planner moves upward. As soon as the protagonist overcomes one conflict, she is hit by another close call.

The Middle of the Middle

The middle of the middle is often where a new and unfamiliar world is deepened. However, even here, the Plot Planner line is not flat but continues steadily rising. Earlier in the middle, the tension may drop off as the protagonist experiences the new world she has entered. From this point on, as your protagonist ascends to the crisis or dark night, if the tension drops off for more than a scene or two, you are likely to lose the reader's attention. Once the reader's mind wanders away from the story, it is more difficult to lure him back into the story.

The protagonist leaves behind the life she knows for the unknown, and new and challenging situations arise. Self-doubts and uncertainty confront the character. She discovers strengths and struggles with shortcomings. She becomes evermore conscious of her thoughts, feelings, and actions, and the shifts from the life she has always known.

A band of antagonists control the middle: other people, nature, society, machines, and the inner demons of the character herself. The antagonists' rhythmic waves of assault spur the protagonist's vertical ascent. The unusual world continues to unfold, and the character begins to undergo a transformation on an inner level long before any observable changes appear.

Characters must make choices, and those choices must create conflict. Cliff-hangers and unexpected twists and turns reflect the rising action of the middle all the way to the crisis. If the plotline is a line of energy, the crisis is the highest point of dramatic action so far in the story, where the protagonist becomes more aware and sensitive. She begins to perceive and experience her life and the world around her in a new way.

Immediately after the crisis, the Plot Planner line falls, giving readers a chance to take a breather.

The Crisis

You will notice that the middle of the Plot Planner line culminates at a high point. This is the crisis, the highest point of tension and conflict in your story thus far and the lowest point in the entire story for the protagonist. This major turning point in the plot serves as a beacon to guide you through the middle.

Each scene in the middle portion of your story marches the protagonist one step closer to the crisis. The protagonist believes she is marching closer and closer to her long-term story goal, so when she gets to the crisis, she may be shocked. The reader, however, has experienced the steady march and feels the inevitability of this moment because of the linkage and causality between each scene and the constantly rising tension of story.

It is only in the darkness of a crisis in our lives—a failure or the death of a loved one or the breakup of a marriage or the loss of a treasured job—that we are forced to see ourselves as we truly are. Toward the end of the middle portion of your story, you want your protagonist to be confronted with her basic character flaw in such a dramatic way that she can no longer remain unconscious of her inner self.

This creates the key question: In knowing her flaw, will the protagonist remain the same or be changed to the core? You know as well as I do that in the heat of battle we say all sorts of things in our attempt to scramble back to our comfort zone. We make pacts with whatever power we believe controls our destiny. We promise to never be so foolhardy or curious or judgmental or angry, so long as we are able to go on, survive, make it past this horrible situation that has triggered such a life-changing wake-up call.

Of course, it is quite another thing to actually follow through on all those promises, once life settles down. For the purposes of your story, don't worry about that yet. For now, all you need to do is create a scene that puts the protagonist in such an uncomfortable, potentially life-threatening or ego-threatening situation that she must finally see herself for who she truly is.

Of course, because the crisis is such a turning point in the story, fraught with tension and conflict and suspense, it has to be written in scene.

If you find yourself quickly summarizing events instead of creating the crisis, stop and ask yourself: Am I shying away from this because the material seems too hard, too long, or too painful to write? If you answered yes to any of these questions, take a deep breath and try writing the events moment by moment. You may find yourself crying or perspiring or swearing at the screen as you write. Do not give up. Keep at it. Dig deep. Use the emotion to fuel your story.

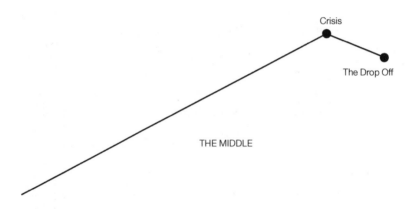

As you will note, after the crisis, the Plot Planner line drops for the first time. This is because after the intensity of the crisis, you want to give your readers an opportunity to rest for a moment, to digest all that has gone on thus far. This is a time for both your reader and your protagonist to reflect on what has transpired. This is a quiet time after the crisis. A story cannot be 100 percent struggle. But, as with other parts of your story, this rest period cannot go on for too long.

In *All the Light We Cannot See*, each chapter in the buildup to the crisis is comprised of one short scene filled with rising tension. The villain, Von Rumpel (who is more than an antagonist because his goal is not simply to block Marie-Laure from her goal but to take what Marie-Laure has) enters the apartment building where Marie-Laure had lived with her father before the invasion and uncovers an important clue to the whereabouts of the object he desires. In the next chapter, Werner, who has become known for his ability to locate enemy transmitters, spots a young girl singing a song he recognizes from the Children's Home where he grew up. Soon after he targets a transmission incorrectly, and as a result, the young girl and her mother are shot and killed. Of the hundred men Werner is responsible for having killed, he is haunted by these two deaths. In the next short scene, a telegraph goes out requesting Werner to go to Saint-Malo, where Marie-Laure lives in the tall house on the shore and enemy transmissions have been detected. That chapter is followed by a summary telling of the first bombs to hit Saint-Malo. In the next chapter, we find Marie-Laure trapped in her house with the villain.

Each of these short scenes builds tension and brings the war and Werner to Marie-Laure. Werner's crisis served to open his eyes to the senseless killing and his part in the slaughter. Marie-Laure's chapter shows her starving and later taking actions that she knows will alert the villain to her whereabouts, which demonstrates her willingness to sacrifice herself for the good of the cause.

▶ PLOT THE MIDDLE

It is time to create the middle portion of your Plot Planner. To get started, retrieve the numbers you generated in chapter three, as well as the Plot Planner you have already begun.

If you have written a rough draft, count the scenes that occur after the end of the beginning, stopping at the number of middle scenes you calculated in chapter three. (For instance, if you calculated thirty scenes for your middle, count out thirty scenes in your rough draft, starting with the scene just after the end of the beginning.) Take a look at where that number puts you in the story. Is this scene the best stopping point for the middle? Does it pop out at you for its high dramatic action? Is it a scene where character emotional development is at its peak? If not, look to the scenes that come before and after. You are looking for the highest point of tension and conflict in the story so far, a true crisis for the protagonist. This scene is the character's darkest moment, her greatest loss, her worst setback, the final blow, the most severe betrayal. Find it? Use that to end the middle of your Plot Planner, even if the scene comes a bit before or after the scene number you counted to. The parameters we set up in chapter three are guidelines only; you don't have to follow them exactly. For now, decide where you believe the middle portion of your story begins (immediately after the end of the beginning) and ends (usually one to five scenes after the crisis).

Unroll twice as much banner paper for the middle as you did for the beginning. Continue the line you started for plotting, making it sweep steadily upward. About six inches from the end of this portion of the banner paper, drop the line down about six inches.

Now start plotting your scenes!

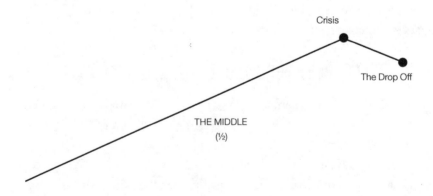

Do not fall into the trap beginning writers often make: Never summarize where a scene is needed.

RAISE THE STAKES

Support the middle with overarching tension by increasing the stakes. For instance, while the protagonist is waiting to hear about whether she will receive funding for an animal preserve before the bank forecloses on her land, torrential rains flood her home and destroy the property. Now that she has nothing, how can she possibly save the animals? When the reader knows something significant is at stake, like the lives of the animals, and that the outcome will be revealed later in the story, he is willing to wait and first learn more about how the exotic world of the middle operates before the physical, psychological, and spiritual crises ensue.

THE DETAILED MIDDLE

One trick to developing scenes for the middle is to develop a subplot around the details of a unique task, job, or setting within the action. Subplots help to reinforce the overall meaning of the story. Readers like to learn new things when they read. For instance, many of the middle scenes of *The Secret Life of Bees* by Sue Monk Kidd involve the processes and trappings of beekeeping. Within the context of the plot, the reader learns all sorts of details about bees and honey while at the same time comes to a deeper understanding of the characters. Similarly the middle of *Balling the Jack* by Frank Baldwin is filled with inside information into the world of high-stakes dart games. E. Annie Proulx sets her novel *The Shipping News* in a remote location that many readers may never have considered: the Newfoundland coast. She fills her scenes in the middle with details of the world of shipping, the tides, and newspaper writing.

Folly by Laurie R. King

This Plot Planner uses symbols to indicate scenes that show character emotional development (≈) and dramatic action (◊).

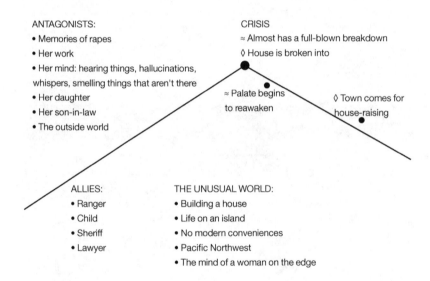

ANTAGONISTS:
- Memories of rapes
- Her work
- Her mind: hearing things, hallucinations, whispers, smelling things that aren't there
- Her daughter
- Her son-in-law
- The outside world

CRISIS
- ≈ Almost has a full-blown breakdown
- ◊ House is broken into

≈ Palate begins
to reawaken

◊ Town comes for
house-raising

ALLIES:
- Ranger
- Child
- Sheriff
- Lawyer

THE UNUSUAL WORLD:
- Building a house
- Life on an island
- No modern conveniences
- Pacific Northwest
- The mind of a woman on the edge

KEY
≈ Character Emotional Development
◊ Dramatic Action

Chapter Eight

PLOT THE DRAMATIC ACTION

Plot is a series of scenes that are deliberately arranged by cause and effect to create *dramatic action* …

Dramatic action creates excitement and urges readers to keep turning pages in a book. Without the presence of drama, action can be considered passive or simply movement. Movement and momentum qualify as action, but movement wrought with conflict, tension, and suspense transforms into dramatic action—which, in turn, engages readers.

DRAMATIC ACTION VS. PASSIVE ACTION

As carefully as you plot the overall dramatic action and sense of uncertainty in your stories, use the same level of scrutiny when tracking the type of action—dramatic versus passive—in each scene to create a sense of expectancy, anticipation, and longing in the reader.

When the protagonist is not in control of the action, this casts doubt about the character's ability to succeed and renders the scene dramatic. If something or someone other than the protagonist is in control of the outcome, the action becomes dramatic and the consequences uncertain: "Will she or won't she get what she wants?" This elevates the intensity of the drama (which is vital for your story), and the reader reads faster to learn the answer.

The term *passive action* may seem like an oxymoron. However, I use this label to identify any habitual action taken by the characters that results in no risk, obstacles, opponents, opposition, danger, uncertainty, or emotion. Passive action scenes fall below the Plot Planner line.

In small doses passive action has its benefits. It can show the character's internal reaction to the external events, slow down the pace of the story, bring a bit of levity when the story becomes too gloomy, demonstrate the character's demeanor when she isn't under stress, reveal a deeper look into her inner life, give her a chance to create a new game plan, and give the reader a chance to breathe.

Some examples of passive action include:

- two characters window shopping and talking
- a character giving a presentation in his field of excellence
- two characters walking on a beach
- a character cooking breakfast and sitting down to eat it

Passive action scenes can also be called contemplative scenes, and they work best when they are short and placed between two dramatic action scenes. Too much passive action and your story stalls and you risk losing your reader's interest.

Drama implies a power imbalance between the character and an antagonist, which creates dark emotions. The degree of imbalance determines the seriousness of the struggle. If, for example, your character is jogging on a city sidewalk, preoccupied by her shopping list, her upcoming meetings, and other mundane thoughts, this is considered action (or movement), but it is not *dramatic* action. Scenes with action of this type belong below the Plot Planner line. Dramatic action means that plenty of conflict, tension, suspense, uncertainty, and/or fear is present in the scene; in other words, drama. Think now of a scene in which your character is being chased by a gunman through grimy alleyways and is unable to think clearly because her fear is so great. This scene is filled with dramatic action and belongs above the Plot Planner line.

Keep these points in mind as you plan dramatic action within your scenes:

- If your protagonist is shown running in a scene, without the presence of drama, the action depicted is simply movement.
- Without the sense of the unknown, the action depicted is simply movement.
- Without great doubt about the character's ability to obtain her goals ("Will she or won't she succeed?"), the action depicted is simply movement.
- Without something or someone other than the protagonist in control of the action, the action depicted is simply movement.

Now that your scenes in the middle are in place, use your Plot Planner to help you determine the pacing of your dramatic action plot.

✏️ TEST SCENES FOR DRAMATIC ACTION

To test whether a scene has dramatic action, ask who controls the action, and likely the outcome, of the scene. Who is stronger and more powerful—the protagonist or the antagonist?

Take, for example, a character with a scene goal of enticing her crazy neighbor out of his house so she can see him for herself and thus win a bet. In this case, the protagonist's fear overrides her curiosity, and she bolts before she can set her goal in motion. By surrendering her control and moving away from her goal, her fear works as an internal antagonist. Thus the scene belongs above the Plot Planner line.

THE PATTERN OF STORIES

Guggenheim Fellow and award-winning novelist Kurt Vonnegut wrote his master's thesis about the pattern of stories. Graphing the ups and downs of characters reveals the classification and arrangement of some of the more common and distinct story and plot types. He wrote: "The fundamental idea is that stories have shapes which can be drawn on graph paper, and that the shape of a given society's stories is at least as interesting as the shape of its pots or spearheads." He believed in plotting on graph paper; I recommend banner paper. Following are two of his classic story shapes.

Man in Hole   Boy Meets Girl

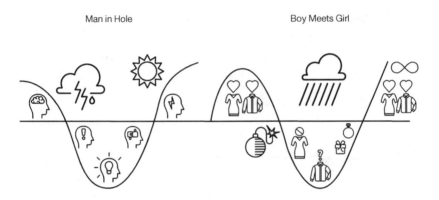

These images depict the crisis, or dark night, of the middle as falling into a hole or dark place. Though the Plot Planner instead traces a line that steadily moves higher, both visuals illustrate trouble. In Vonnegut's graph, the main character's circumstances of good fortune are plotted above ground while the line below reflects his ill fortune.

The Plot Planner line reflects the energy of the story rising in intensity scene by scene. That intensity is created by an antagonist's good fortune causing the protagonist ill fortune. Both methods, though polar opposite reflections, are telling the same story—someone wants something, is interfered with, overcomes the opposition, and ends up better off than where they started.

Plot your story ideas on a Plot Planner with the action itself in mind for now. For each scene, simply determine if your protagonist is struggling against something or someone who wields more power, experience, wisdom, knowledge, skills, abilities, or favor, or if she is relatively in control. If she begins the scene in control, sure of what she is doing and where she is going, and she ends the scene in trouble, consider that entire scene as an above-the-line scene.

You'll find scenes that fall short, do not meet the criteria, plummet below the Plot Planner line or, in Vonnegut's story shapes, sit at ground level. For help in creating and plotting more tension and conflict in your scenes, see chapter nine.

GENERATING MORE DRAMATIC ACTION

If your scenes currently lack dramatic action, there are a number of ways to inject them with more.

1. Call in the antagonists:

    - Friends, family, or co-workers can stir up conflict for the protagonist.
    - A natural disaster could be the problem your protagonist must face.
    - A physical disability could hinder the protagonist from reaching his goal.
    - The rules of religion, government, and customs might interfere with the protagonist's needs or desires.
    - The protagonist's car could break down on the way to an important event.
    - The protagonist's motorcycle could skid on a slippery road.
    - The protagonist could battle fears, flaws, or prejudice—either personal or that of others.
    - The protagonist could face a ticking clock.
    - Know the climax to help determine which antagonists are needed for the story in anticipation of what's coming.

2. Use foreshadowing in the middle to introduce overarching tension, conflict, or suspense in the plot.
3. Delve more deeply into the character's emotional development by detailing her reactions to the opposition she meets.
4. When you test your scenes for cause and effect, ask yourself: Because this happens, what happens next? Also explore ideas that flow seamlessly from the scenes that came before and then twist the action in a seemingly impossible direction, complicating the character's circumstances and thwarting reader expectations. For instance, the character (and the reader) believes she has identified the murderer, but on her way to confront the bad guy, she discovers his corpse.
5. Don't reveal everything at once. Leave hints and spread out the need-to-know details. Milk the suspense of the unknown. Curiosity drives the reader deeper into the story to learn the answers to the whys and hows you present.
6. Add a great subplot like a relationship that thematically complements the primary plot and adds interest and complexity.
7. Crescendo scenes in the middle with action and drama at the crisis that tops all the other setbacks and complications.

Right after the intensity of the crisis, the energy of the story drops off for a bit to allow the protagonist to catch his or her breath.

Chapter Nine

PLOT THE TENSION AND CONFLICT

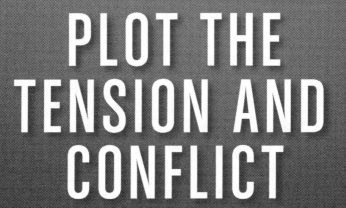

Plot is a series of scenes that are deliberately arranged by cause and effect to create dramatic action filled with *tension and conflict …*

Conflicts are serious disagreements, arguments, opposition, clashes, battles, disputes, problems, squabbles, and dissension between two or more disparate parties. Conflicts in stories cause characters to feel threatened (physically or emotionally, or by the potential loss of power or status) and to react to protect their needs, interests, concerns, and well-being.

A situation with an uncertain outcome, in which two or more characters are in conflict, creates tension. Tension is the mental or emotional strain caused by conflict. When characters who are at odds are involved in ongoing relationships, they struggle, discover they are incompatible, dispute various issues, differ in opinion, collide, contrast, and generate tension between each other.

In fiction, conflicts rivet the reader's attention and create tension, suspense, and curiosity about the outcome. It's the unknown that carries the reader deeper and deeper into the story. Every time you satisfy the reader's curiosity in a scene or plotline, her attention wanes. To avoid this, continue introducing new or foreshadowed conflicts.

Like a game of leapfrog, you will move your reader from one major conflict to the next.

AVOID MAKING IT TOO EASY

If you love your protagonist, you may be tempted to make it too easy for her to get what she wants, find success, snag her lover, or solve the mystery. If this is the case, your story might begin with her overcoming every conflict and squashing every opponent. Your reader will quickly understand that in the hands of the protagonist, there is nothing to fear and all will end well. Continue in this way and by the middle of the story, your reader will become distracted and bored.

On the other hand, if you love your readers and are eager to make fans, make it hard for your protagonist to succeed. Trip her up, embarrass her, humiliate her, scare her, intimidate her, and challenge her to the point that the reader is never quite sure what will happen next in the story and has to turn the pages faster in order to find out.

The protagonist may have started the story believing she can achieve the life she'd always dreamed of. No matter how prepared she may have been for the challenges ahead of her, she has no idea to what extent she will be stretched, of the conflicts she will face, or of the risks involved. If she did, she may not seize the chance to achieve something great in life, as she is too frightened to take the initial leap.

As with any risk, there is always something at stake. Risk implies that along with great riches, the protagonist also stands to lose greatly—her money, time, and/or reputation are threatened. Risk also implies tension. The reader is forced to read on to find out what happens next.

THE BENEFITS OF TAKING RISKS

Forcing your protagonist to take risks opens him up to new challenges and opportunities to learn a new skill, language, belief, or way of living.

Readers may do everything they can to prevent risks, upheaval, loss, bad times, tension, and stress from entering their own lives. Yet they're quite satisfied to read about conflicts and to vicariously experience the characters' drama. They read to live on an edge and in a state of heightened tension they'd never risk in their real lives.

Taking risks empowers the protagonist to break through limited thoughts and beliefs, which in turn has the potential to challenge readers to ponder those same limits in themselves. When a character has a misconstrued vision of what he thinks he deserves or is capable of accomplishing, he'll never know the reality unless he risks the chance of failure to venture out into new territory.

Risk creates tension—as well as reward. When a character takes risks and goes out on a limb, the reader is better able to assess his natural problem-solving skills under tension, to learn more about his strengths and weaknesses when confronted with obstacles, and to invest emotional energy in him by worrying about his welfare and safety.

Taking risks helps the protagonist more clearly define what he truly wants. Is the reward worth taking the chance? Is there something else he'd rather work toward? Those same risks allow the reader to predict the best course of action for the protagonist and read further to measure the outcome.

Tension is created in not knowing for sure if the risks the character takes will eliminate negative thinking in the end and lead him to excel even beyond what he initially set out to achieve. Whether the character ultimately succeeds, fails, or experiences something else entirely is a question that draws the reader deeper into the story.

The more and greater risks the protagonist is willing to take, the greater the potential conflict and tension as he breaks from his usual way of living and thinking. Instead of resisting the struggle, ignoring the antagonist, and fighting to stay safe, he accepts what comes and gains the momentum and confidence needed to face his antagonists and his fears.

With your scenes plotted on your Plot Planner, now turn your focus from the protagonist to the goals of the major antagonists.

✏️ ADD ANTAGONISTS TO THE PLOT PLANNER

Antagonists are simply characters whose goals interfere with the protagonist's goals. Keep in mind that the antagonist has his own goals and makes his way, step by step, toward them. In so doing, he either deliberately or unknowingly creates obstacles for the protagonist.

There are two primary methods for plotting the antagonist's plotlines:

1. If the antagonist is a major character and/or a villain, give the character her own Plot Planner line, positioned below the primary Plot Planner line.
2. If the antagonist is a minor important character, give him his own colored sticky note to plot his scenes on the main Plot Planner line.

With either method, plot the antagonist's plotline in much the same way you did for the protagonist's plot.

As you move forward, consider goals for the antagonists that directly or indirectly hinder, hamper, stall, prevent, or delay the protagonist from moving easily toward his own goal.

In the middle, use as many antagonists as you need in order to prevent the protagonist from achieving his long-term goal. In other words, use the protagonist's family, friends, co-workers, enemies, and lovers to thwart his progress. When appropriate, throw in a natural disaster or a physical disability to slow down the protagonist's quest. Let the protagonist's religion or government or customs forbid him from continuing. Have the protagonist's car break down at just the right moment, or have a motorcycle skid to a stop at just the wrong moment. Have the protagonist's inner life, past mistakes, fears, flaws, doubts, moral choices, or lack of willpower constantly get in his way. Introduce a time limit to amp up the pressure. Present a sense of danger.

Whatever it takes, create middle scenes to slow down or even stop the protagonist's journey toward his goal. Set up anticipation on the part of the protagonist and the reader, and then drag out the suspense—will he or won't he achieve his goal? Prolong the tension (though be sure to provide an equal payoff). Plot the antagonist's scenes on your Plot Planner using each of these techniques to ensure that the stakes escalate in each subsequent scene.

As the protagonist pushes toward something, see that forces both internal and external interfere with his progress. It is in the struggle between the protagonist and all the antagonists, all the conflicts, and all the tension that creates action on the page. This, in turn, forces readers to read faster in excitement and expectation, spurred onward by their morbid curiosity, trepidation, anticipation, and intense longing.

Look at the scenes you have placed above the Plot Planner line, and ask what is causing the tension and conflict, scene by scene. Is it another person, an animal, nature, machines, or perhaps society? Is the placement consistent with the flow of energy from scene to scene as you build to each major turning point? Does the tension drop off afterward, only to build even higher as the protagonist moves further into the story?

The Antagonist's Climax

As you plot the antagonist's plotline, watch how it influences the protagonist's plotline in the buildup to the crisis and during the crisis. During the buildup, antagonists often grow in power and control, and create more tension and intense conflicts as the protagonist slips or fools herself into believing she's near the end. Think of the *crisis*, which generally occurs around three-quarters into the entire project, as the climax of the antagonist's plotline.

That's not to say that the antagonist crushes the protagonist and then departs in victory. Whatever happens to the antagonist at this point in the story fuels his passion to continue for more or greater influence, control, possessions, power, accolades, and attention. Thus the conflicts and tension build. This means that when the protagonist enters the end of the story, she's moving forward to face an even more powerful force.

There are two other ways to look at the crisis of the story:

1. The crisis is the protagonist's moment of truth; afterwards nothing is ever the same. In other words, she is confronted with a twist in the action she had not anticipated. For instance, the alleged murderer she has been pursuing becomes a victim, and she realizes that the cold-blooded killer is still at large.
2. In the crisis, the protagonist has a breakdown that leads to a breakthrough. In other words, she is confronted by her personal demons and is forced to face the truth that no outside force landed her in the mess she's in—her own stubbornness, naiveté, anger, carelessness, or procrastination did.

INTRODUCING PLOT TWISTS

Plot twists engage readers. Twist the dramatic action in an unexpected (and carefully foreshadowed) direction so the protagonist is forced to define new goals and perform difficult tasks while pointing the reader in the direction of her true goal.

At each of the major turning points in your story, imagine and list five horrible antagonists that create five horrible events for the protagonist. Look for people and actions that feel the most thematically true to the protagonist's ultimate transformation *and* that twist the story in a new (and carefully foreshadowed) direction. The Plot Planner guides the direction and degree of the story's intensity and provides a place for expansion. Each horrible thing broadens the reader's appreciation of the protagonist's sense of self beyond the limitations of what was currently visible in the story.

Horror writers penetrate our deepest fears and bring darkness to light. In real life, most of us run from or at least avoid the dark. We're afraid of the unknown and always looking for the light. We deny our negative feelings and deny our protagonists their shadows. We attempt to navigate the straight and narrow line of the Plot Planner, afraid of losing control of the story and falling into an abyss.

The braver you are, the bigger your story. Rather than confuse the reader, use each plot twist to spin the story deeper into the darkness of what haunts the protagonist, urges him to take heart and gather his courage for his next defined test of initiation, and, in the end, brings to light his true personal power.

At each major point of conflict, name the protagonist's emotion as she anticipates the conflict, as the conflict is happening, and in the aftermath of the conflict. Search for the truth in her emotions. Convey that step, that emotion, in an active, energetic, and meaningful way that fulfills the three major plotlines:

- character emotional development plot: defines the emotion
- dramatic action plot: shows steps taken and resistance met
- thematic significance plot: defines that action and the meaning of her emotion

The straight and well-defined line of the Plot Planner is an attempt to control the twisty and often blurry reality in stories. Each dark twist and turn defines the protagonist's next specific short-term goal. Imagine the next horrible thing, obstacle, challenge, or demon your protagonist meets. Foreshadow and twist the forward action in yet a different direction that affords a new view of him. Show emotions that are thematically true to his character.

Each time an antagonist twists the story in a new direction, the protagonist defines a new goal like an arrow flying in the direction that brings forward her true purpose, releases power, and provides her the freedom to conquer her fears and align with the final confrontation in her willingness to transform.

INTENSIFYING THE CONFLICT AND TENSION

As you consider the placement of your middle scenes either above or below the Plot Planner line, ask yourself the following questions at the overall plot and story level:

- Where are the major conflicts?
- Who are the conflicts primarily between?
- What is causing the conflict?
- How much tension is caused by the conflict?
- Does the tension in your story as a whole agree with the expected tension in your genre? For instance, the tension in a suspense novel should skyrocket to the climax. In women's fiction, the tension will simmer but won't match the intensity of the suspense genre.

Chapter Ten

PLOT THE END

The fact that you survived the middle, whether you limped your way through it or leapt over the obstacles and the unknowns, is cause for celebration. Go ahead—beat your chest and proclaim to the world that you plotted your way through the murky, meddlesome, and messy middle. Now we must continue onward, to the final leg of the journey.

As unbelievable as it might seem, you are in the homestretch, the final quarter of your story.

THE FALSE SUMMIT

As your character reached the crisis, she thought her problems were over—that is, until she caught a glimpse of the even higher mountain still quite a distance away. She then realized she was only at the false summit. So how do you and she make it to that next peak, the true summit? Step by step, just like you made it to the crisis.

Often in life, we make pacts with whatever power we believe controls our destiny, so long as we are able to go on, survive another day, or make it past this horrible event that has triggered such a life-changing wake-up call. Yet once life settles down and the fear has vanished, somehow we forget our promises. Your protagonist likely does the same thing. Now, just past the false summit, we need to address this universal character reaction.

For your story, this pact-making happens in the scenes at the very end of the middle, when the intensity of the story wanes for a bit to give the reader and the protagonist time to rest and make plans.

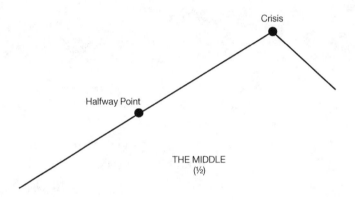

In your first draft, focus chiefly on getting your story down on paper. In subsequent rewrites you can be more creative.

THE TRUE SUMMIT

Your protagonist has been confronted with an uncomfortable, potentially life-threatening or ego-demoralizing situation and finally sees himself for who he actually is—flaws and all. In the middle of your story, through all the opposition he encounters, as well as through his downfall, he also gains strength, logic, clues, and skills he only becomes aware of after the crisis. Having survived, he is also more confident. In the last quarter of the story, he has to make a decision. Is he going to rationalize his way out of change, shoving his promises to a dark corner of her mind? Or does he accept the challenge to move from his comfort zone and risk the unknown to live his life differently from this point forward? You decide—or let your protagonist decide. Whatever the answer, it is up to you, the writer, to create scenes in this final quarter of your story that will allow the protagonist to make choices, whereby "showing" the reader which direction he is moving.

You get to decide if your protagonist will beat the odds and succeed in changing permanently. The only way to show that is by creating scenes that give the protagonist the opportunity to make choices. You have one-quarter of the total number of scenes (or one-quarter of the total number of pages of your entire book) in which to do this.

THE LIGHT SWITCHES ON

Think of the middle as the tunnel of darkness, fraught with antagonists of all sorts. The crisis is the dark night of the soul, in which the protagonist hits rock bottom and becomes conscious of who she really is, or of what she has been avoiding or denying. Because of what happens at the crisis, a light snaps on, and thus begins the process of transformation.

In the End, the protagonist still has foes to confront and overcome, but now she is empowered with a new understanding of herself and/or her circumstances. For the first time, her true goal comes into focus.

In the end, the Plot Planner line flies nearly straight upward to the climax, the crowning glory of the entire piece. The end is half as long as the middle, which means the conflicts and obstacles must rise quickly, one after another. Here, at the end, the tension is at its greatest as the protagonist struggles to take full ownership of her newly discovered consciousness. In the quick buildup to the climax, the protagonist more keenly recognizes that her actions or speech do not align with her new understanding of herself and the world around her.

As she nears her goal, the obstacles constitute increasing levels of difficulty. The end unfolds, one scene into the next, in a deliberate and calculated way. It must not be predictable, but it must be inevitable. In the end you must deliver the promise you made in the beginning.

This is not the place to stop for a flashback or backstory or explanation. This is the place to quickly build momentum. So long as you have not raised the stakes too high or too soon, you can now escalate the action as you reach the climax.

⫸ PLOT THE END

To create the end portion of your Plot Planner, retrieve the numbers you generated in chapter three and the Plot Planner you have already begun.

After the protagonist has integrated what's necessary, rid him of what no longer serves him, including limited beliefs about himself and life around him. If he has established a plan, no matter how sketchy or vague, he's ready to move forward. The end begins when he takes the first step toward his final goal.

On the Plot Planner, decide where you believe the end of your story should be placed. Expose only the part of the paper you will be working on for now. Continue the line you have started, making it sweep steadily upward from the drop-off point. Bring it to the highest peak thus far and then drop the line down about half a foot.

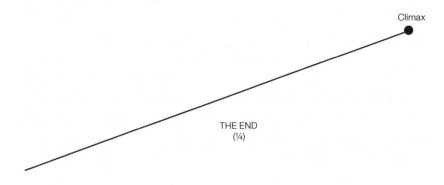

The mini-breather you created, which allowed both your reader and your protagonist to recover from the crisis and reflect, is over. Now it is time to start cranking up the tension and the conflicts again. Start plotting your scenes. The end is near. The stakes are high.

Once you know how the character is going to play out the final confrontation, you have all you need to know.

The Climax

Each scene in the steady trek to the end builds in significance and relevance through rising tension and conflict until your protagonist reaches the true summit, the climax of the entire story. This is where she is confronted by the biggest hurdle, the greatest challenge, and the toughest test. Will she react and revert back to her old, habitual ways, flaws and all? Or will she embrace her newly discovered power and show the world that she is a changed person all the way to her core? Will she get what she wants? Now that she has what she thinks she wants, is she satisfied? What has she learned?

The climax serves as the protagonist's light at the end of the tunnel (and, as the joke goes, it's not a train). He moves toward the light: one step forward, toward the ultimate transformation, and then two steps back as he struggles and is beaten backwards. Often in the middle, the protagonist moves in much the same way, taking one or more steps forward before being pushed back. At the end, after all he has learned, he still is pushed back, but now, rather than bulldozing his way forward with blinders on and little care for who he tramples, he assesses the situation from all sides, always on the lookout for the next *unexpected* step he believes will take him to his goal. In the middle, he was driven by success. In the end, he is driven by the desire to finish what he started. The protagonist has been empowered by the knowledge gained at the crisis. He has learned the rules of the game. He is wiser and more powerful. Therefore, the obstacles must be made more difficult scene by scene. Setbacks should continue to plague him, and the challenges should intensify.

The climax spotlights the character in full transformation demonstrating necessary new skills, personality traits, gifts, or actions to achieve her goal. She acts in scene in a transformed way—in a way she could not have acted in any other part of the story, because she first needed to experience everything she does in the book to get to the final stage.

The protagonist demonstrates the transformation she underwent in the story by doing something in the climax she was unable to do at the beginning of the story.

This final scene does not have to be an all-out war, full of explosions and death. It *does* have to contain meaning to the overall story.

When you know how the story ends, you then know every moment that must be dramatized to create a convincing and meaningful climax. Work backward from the climax, and dig for motivation behind every action, the purpose of every scene, and the significance of every detail to bring the story to that moment. Every word leads the reader to the inevitable, but still surprising, conclusion. All scenes must be thematically or structurally justified in the light of the climax.

If a scene does not contribute to the climax, see if you can strengthen its cause and its effect. If not, then ask yourself if it can be cut without disturbing the impact of the ending. Once you have shed the dead weight of unnecessary scenes, arrange all your remaining scenes and details as "whispers" to prepare the reader for the climax. The reader may hope against hope for a certain outcome, but when he gets there, it should be obvious that there was absolutely no other possible ending than the one you have written.

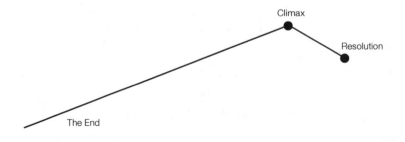

WRITING BLOCKBUSTER PLOTS

THE RESOLUTION

Once the protagonist shows the mastery of what is needed in the climax, the line drops for the Resolution. The Resolution is usually a brief tying up of most of the loose ends. If the story resonates with thematic significance (see chapter thirteen), the reader is left to ponder the deeper meaning.

It is best not to have the Resolution go on for too long, and there is no need to resolve all the plotlines. The energy of the story has dropped, and as much as the reader does not want the story to end, it is up to you to end it. Prolong the resolution and your story becomes like the last guest to leave the party, a little woozy and worn-out.

THE WHOLE STORY

Now that you have the entire Plot Planner drawn out and organized, take a bit of time to view the story as a whole. Writing for discovery without first planning a plot may benefit creativity, but without a clear idea of where your story is taking you, this method can quickly lead you astray. Now that you have scene ideas plotted out on your Plot Planner, they may change, move, and grow as you write and continue plotting. Even so, with a plot plan in place, you can write from the beginning and plot to the end in a way that supports both your logic and your imagination rather than wandering down dead-ends and dark alleyways for months.

As I said earlier in this chapter, the end sets up the crowning glory of the entire story—the climax. This scene shows the character fully united with her new self-knowledge, her new understanding of the world, and her new sense of responsibility through her actions and her words. Now that you know what the action is at the climax, evaluate how it ties to the beginning and the middle. Then deliberately plot from the end by deconstructing who the character becomes due to the conflicts and learning that take place in the middle.

At the climax of *Folly*, a mystery novel by the award-winning Laurie R. King, the protagonist, in an effort to protect not only herself but her granddaughter, stands up to a man with a gun who has been terrorizing her. That this character begins the novel fragile and paranoid, and ready to commit suicide on a remote island, adds depth and meaning to the final confrontation. In the middle, she tosses her antidepressant pills and pushes herself physically, all the while having hallucinations and hearing whispers. At the crisis, she suffers a full-blown panic attack. Each of these earlier major plot points serves to bring more meaning, excitement, and emotional investment to the final confrontation at the climax, which involves so much more than simply stopping the bad guy. The climax is where the protagonist shows herself to be healed.

Folly by Laurie R. King

This Plot Planner uses symbols to indicate scenes that show character emotional development (≈) and dramatic action (◊).

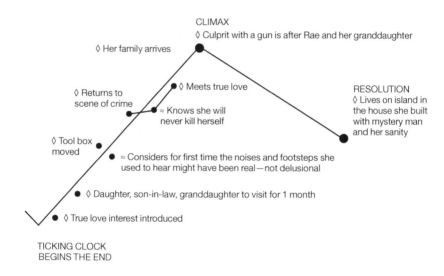

CLIMAX
◊ Culprit with a gun is after Rae and her granddaughter

◊ Her family arrives

◊ Meets true love

◊ Returns to
scene of crime

≈ Knows she will
never kill herself

RESOLUTION
◊ Lives on island in
the house she built
with mystery man
and her sanity

◊ Tool box
moved

≈ Considers for first time the noises and footsteps she
used to hear might have been real—not delusional

◊ Daughter, son-in-law, granddaughter to visit for 1 month

◊ True love interest introduced

TICKING CLOCK
BEGINS THE END

KEY
≈ Character Emotional Development
◊ Dramatic Action

Chapter Eleven

CREATE THE CHARACTER EMOTIONAL DEVELOPMENT PROFILE

> Plot is a series of scenes that are deliberately arranged by cause and effect to create dramatic action filled with conflict to further *character emotional development* ...

Most popular fiction is 30 percent dramatic action and 70 percent emotional character development. Dramatic action excites readers. More important, readers connect and, at best, emotionally bond with the characters. To make the most of this emotional connection and deepen the relationship between reader and characters, the characters must be relatable on some level. Commonly that relatability comes through the character's goals, motivation, and character traits. However, a relatable character is not enough. Rather than remain static and unchanged, the character must grow and further her emotional development in response to what happens to her throughout the story. The Character Emotional Development Profile asks you to consider each of these pivotal aspects of creating a memorable character.

The first part of the profile covers the external aspects of the character through her goal setting. The character's goal, as well as the reasons for having it, speak volumes about her emotional development at each part the story. As she changes, what drives and motivates her changes, too.

The second part of the profile covers the internal aspects of the character and her emotional development through her personality traits and ultimate transformation.

In this chapter, with the help of *Where the Heart Is* by Billie Letts, I take you through a technique that helps deepen a story's overall plot by focusing on the character emotional development through the goals the protagonist sets for herself.

Your protagonist (and, for that matter, all your characters) has an immediate goal for every scene and an overall story goal. These goals help to develop the front story, the story that is unfolding moment by moment in scene.

A mini-plot of goal, conflict, and disaster makes up a scene, similar to the overall plot structure of a story. Each scene needs an immediate goal. (I discuss the pattern of scenes in further detail in Part Two.)

In *Where the Heart Is*, Letts alludes to Novalee's immediate goal in the first paragraph of the book and then six paragraphs later establishes that her immediate goal is to use a bathroom.

This simple goal works because Novalee is desperate. She is seven months pregnant and her bladder is "like a water balloon."

The author goes on to establish the long-term, overall goal for the entire story at the top of page 5—to live in a house like the pictures she collects from magazines. Novalee's mother walked out on her when she was seven years old, and she has never had a home that was not on wheels.

Sometimes, the long-term, overall story goal is drawn from something the protagonist dreams of having. Dreams are things we wish for, things we enjoy thinking about, but not necessarily things we can attain. Goals are derived from dreams, but the difference is that goals are under our control—they are quantifiable and measurable—while dreams involve a bit of magic.

For instance, if your goal is to finish your book, you can do specific things toward accomplishing this, all of which are under your control. However, if your dream is to be published, a bit of magic is needed. An agent and/or an editor needs to become entranced by your story—and while you can improve your chances of that happening by submitting a stellar story and acting in a professional manner, their involvement is ultimately out of your control. The marketplace must be ready for your product, and there are other considerations and factors in play that influence an agent's or editor's decision. In short, the stars must be aligned to make your dream come true.

Short-term goals are specific things your protagonist has decided she needs to accomplish within a clearly defined period of time.

DEVELOPING CHARACTER EMOTIONAL DEVELOPMENT

As much as the protagonist's goal helps define and develop him emotionally, his internal traits, habits, and repetitive patterns delve more deeply into his emotional development. The protagonist must be drawn as a complex individual with both strengths and weaknesses. The following five traits influence the plot more than any other and have a direct effect on the character's success and failure in the story.

1. Character Flaw

A character flaw is an effective and powerful roadblock in the protagonist's journey toward her short-term and overall goals.

The protagonist's goals set up the action for the scene. Tension is immediately established because the reader has something to worry about. Will the protagonist achieve her immediate goal? Is she getting closer to achieving her overall story goal, scene by scene and chapter by chapter? By now, you know that the more obstacles you toss in the path of the character's journey, the more tension and conflict you create in a scene.

Beyond the people in his life or the outside world (or both), what better way to achieve conflict and tension than to craft an internal flaw, fault, or belief that stands in the way of his immediate goals?

The character acts toward his goal, only to have something inside of himself, react in a way that blocks his success.

In *Where the Heart Is*, Willy Jack stands in the way of Novalee's immediate goal by refusing to stop the car so she can use the bathroom. Her success is blocked. Tension is created. Now it is up to Novalee to decide what to do next.

Novalee's character flaw is that she does not speak up for herself. As soon as Willy Jack abandons Novalee, we witness her inability to ask for help. This is a powerful deterrent toward her meeting with success.

To create tension and conflict, the goal must be important to the protagonist. She must stand to lose something if she is not successful. There needs to be some sort of risk involved. For Novalee, if she is not able to stop soon to relieve herself, well, you know what will happen next. Yet, even though we know what she needs in the first paragraph of the story, she does not speak up until page 6 out of fear of angering Willy Jack.

Novalee's character flaw of not speaking up for herself takes on universal appeal, because it is a common flaw that many people share.

The following are examples of common flaws you can utilize for your character's development:

- drinks too much
- dishonest
- judgmental
- insecure
- bullheaded
- selfish
- spends too much money
- negative
- gambles
- victim
- dishonest
- blames others instead of taking responsibility
- worries too much

- egotistical
- gossips
- narcissistic
- procrastinates
- thief
- violent temper
- naïve
- cheater
- disloyal
- unfaithful
- addictive personality

Or pick one of your own flaws—we all have them—and then exaggerate it.

Your goal is to establish in readers an affinity and affection for your protagonist.

---

2. Character Strength

To offset the protagonist's flaw, she must also have strength. A protagonist cannot be passive; she must have some character strength to give the reader at least a hint that she is capable of overcoming her flaw, or at least of becoming conscious of it.

Story is struggle, and so the protagonist must have the strength to fight against all odds and brave the conflicts she faces. Every time the protagonist's will is overwhelmed, she must gather her strength and fight back.

Novalee is intelligent and kind. She is tough, and more than anything else, she is a survivor. Her kindness and acceptance earn her friends. Her survival skills and intelligence support her in outfoxing store management as she creates a home for herself and her unborn baby in the middle of a Walmart store.

3. Hates

It is best if the protagonist feels strongly about the people, places, and events that make up his world. The emotion of hate carries with it a great deal of energy. Hate creates drama, conflict, and tension, which are the building blocks of plot in fiction and memoir. Hate gives the protagonist direction, gets him going, moves him, invigorates him, revs him up, brings him to life, gives him power and strength.

Novalee hates people feeling sorry for her, which is why she does not speak up for herself. In her attempt to protect herself from pity, she often misses rich opportunities for help and guidance, opting to go it alone.

4. Loves

For a reader to sympathize with your protagonist, your character must show that he has feelings. Something in life must make him happy or bring him satisfaction. By showing that your protagonist cares about something or someone special, your reader will better be able to empathize with him. By establishing what the protagonist loves and then by threatening that thing or person, the protagonist is forced to move. Sparks fly.

Novalee loves babies and nice people. But most of all, she loves taking pictures. Photography was her favorite class in high school. The author establishes this love in the first four pages of the book. This love ends up playing a major role in the overall plot by helping her speak up for herself when it most counts.

5. Fears

Fear is a powerful way to create tension and suspense. All of us are afraid of something. By establishing fear in your protagonist, you create a thread of universality. There are many kinds of fear: fear of failure, fear of responsibility, fear of the unknown, fear of the dark. Fear generally paralyzes us, which is why your protagonist needs to embody not just fear but many different emotions. That way, the reader is assured that the protagonist will indeed react.

In *Where the Heart Is*, Novalee fears her boyfriend. This sets up tension on the first page of the book. She also is superstitious about the number seven, which sets up tension. Every time the number is mentioned, the reader feels Novalee tense up in anticipation of disaster. She is also afraid she may be unlovable and unworthy of love, which adds to her reluctance in reaching out to others.

CHARACTER EMOTIONAL DEVELOPMENT ON THE PLOT PLANNER

The protagonist's emotions and psychology give depth and meaning to your story.

Go back to the beginning scenes you plotted in chapter five. Mark the scenes that show the character emotional development. Through the duration of the story, the character will develop from one who is unconscious of her flaws and strengths to a fully actualized (or at least more conscious) protagonist.

▷ FILL OUT THE CHARACTER EMOTIONAL DEVELOPMENT FORM

Following is a form to fill out for your protagonist; it also helps if you fill one out for the villain or antagonist. This way the antagonist, if it is a person, will be a three-dimensional, interesting character rather than a flat cliché. Fill out a form for each secondary character to discover more angles to develop in the story.

As you fill out the form for your protagonist, pause before you jot down each answer. The answer that comes to you first may be superficial. In waiting and inviting the protagonist in, a deeper, more compelling answer may come to you.

CHARACTER EMOTIONAL/PSYCHOLOGICAL PLOT INFORMATION

Protagonist's name:

What is your protagonist's overall story goal?

What stands in his or her way?

What does he or she stand to lose, if not successful (risk)?

What is his or her biggest flaw or fault? Greatest strength?

What does he or she hate? Love? Fear? What secrets does he or she keep from others?

Note: Please refer to Appendix IV for an example of a completed form.

Chapter Twelve

PLOT THE CHARACTER EMOTIONAL DEVELOPMENT

The character who is the most changed or transformed by the action of the story is the protagonist. This character's emotional development as she experiences events and ordeals, successes and failures is one of the three primary plotlines. The challenging situations (the dramatic action plotline) create emotional upheaval and force self-confrontation with a transformation from within (the character emotional development plotline) that creates lasting meaning for the reader (the thematic significance plotline).

Not all characters are transformed by the dramatic action. Plot the characters who do change or transform on your Plot Planner, and track their trait changes on your Scene Tracker (see Part Two). Choose one character to start with, and, throughout the story, plot, explore, and develop that character's emotional makeup. Readers relate to and bond with a character who reveals at the climax that all the events of the story had an emotional impact on her.

The Plot Planner line follows the energy of the story but does *not* reflect or follow the character's emotional development. The line moves steadily upward to reflect rising tension and intensifying conflict in the overall story. When the line reaches the crisis, one of the highest peaks in the story, the character is at her lowest and poorest. If the Plot Planner line did follow the protagonist's fate—which it does not—the line would careen down into the abyss at this point of crisis. Instead the Plot Planner stretches higher and higher and reaches a peak at her breaking point. The line swinging upward in this way reflects the urgency for each scene to present more twisted tension, severe complications, nasty conflict, brutal suspense, and crushing curiosity than occurred in previous scenes.

Plot out on your plot planner the incrementally worse interactions the protagonist encounters. Notice how and where he is most emotionally affected by the dramatic action. The tension and the conflict build as the Plot Planner line rises and the character struggles.

The character's emotional development is most affected at the story's three highest points: the end of the beginning, the crisis, and the climax. Each of these three high points, found in the beginning, middle, and end respectively, creates significantly higher tension than the one that came before, and each demands of the protagonist significantly greater sacrifice, bravery, and stamina to continue in the face of such emotional challenges.

In the first quarter of Doerr's novel *All the Light We Cannot See*, young Werner desperately wishes he could "get away from here." Werner's private fear of going into the mines and dying like his father provides powerful motivation for him to take action. Werner's fear of the life he came from also helps for thematic significance by tying his character emotional development plot to the dramatic action plot. His proclivity for inventing and fixing things (his character strength) also ties into the coming action and provides more meaning by introducing the bigger and more universal idea of inventing something new.

Throughout the middle of the story, the primary gatekeepers to Werner's freedom confront him: his sister, his poverty, the horrors of war, and, ultimately, himself. Through dramatic action, each antagonist teaches Werner about himself and about life, science, the cruelty crouched in men's hearts, and the nature of heroism.

In the final quarter of the story, Werner, having never taken responsibility for what he was doing and his part in the war, comes face-to-face with a blind woman who has personally taken on the responsibility to win the war. Witnessing her boldness, grace, and ultimate heroism, Werner is changed to his core. By staying where he is needed and helping her to safety, he defies reader expectations and becomes the hero of his own life.

Using the Plot Planner template and colored sticky notes, plot the scenes in the beginning quarter of your project either above or below the line, depending on whether the character is in control (below the line) or an antagonist of some sort holds the power over your character (above the line). Note the aspects of the character emotional development introduced: the flaws, fears, and secrets the character possesses. Use a different color sticky note from the color you used for the dramatic action plotline.

In our earlier example, *Folly*, Rae, the protagonist, is introduced as fragile, doubtful, exhausted, and fearful upon her arrival at the island. If we were to plot this on the Plot Planner, we would write "arrival on island" on one colored sticky note above the Plot Planner line for the dramatic action plotline. The note goes above the line because life alone on the remote island is perilous. In a different-colored sticky note at the same place, we would write "fragile and fearful" to indicate Rae's character emotional development at this point.

Feeling fragile, fearful, and on the edge is not a temporary emotional state. These traits make up Rae's lifetime emotional development due to what has come before (her backstory).

The middle section contains scenes both above and below the Plot Planner line that show how the character's current emotional development affects her life on a deeper level. In the middle, make shorthand notes about her emotional development. Jot down notes about how her internal antagonists—her fears, flaws, and secrets—sabotage her and prevent her from reaching her goals.

CHARACTER EMOTIONAL DEVELOPMENT PROFILE
CHARACTER'S NAME: Rae

CHARACTER EMOTIONAL DEVELOPMENT PLOTLINE

FLAWS: suspicious, reactive, jumps to conclusions, on the edge

FEARS: going permanently insane, killing self

STRENGTHS: resolve, discipline, stubbornness, strong will

HATES: being scared

LOVES: granddaughter, working with wood

DREAM: to be normal

SECRET: for a moment, she felt the possibility of killing her child

In *Folly*, during the crisis—the scene of highest intensity in the story so far—Rae has a full-blown breakdown, something she has feared and attempted to prevent with pills and then with hard work. The pressure of the work she undertakes on the island, her fear of the dark and the unknown, and her paranoia create the crisis by forcing her directly into the belly of what she fears the most: being out of control. This time of intense vulnerability serves as a wake-up call, a moment of no return. She now understands the extent of her fragility, but she is also given a glimpse into who she could be with focused and conscious effort. (The sticky note for the crisis is always above the line at the highest peak on the Plot Planner so far.)

The end shows her character emotional development in terms of the degree to which she maintains control as she works her way to mastery. The moment of true mastery is shown in the climax.

In essence, the sticky notes containing character emotional development on the Plot Planner should show a visual pattern of the character emotional development arc.

PACING THE CHARACTER EMOTIONAL DEVELOPMENT

Begin by focusing your attention on reaching the first scene or cluster of scenes with the highest intensity in the story so far: the end of the beginning.

Control the pacing of what you introduce about the character and the effects the action has on her emotions at the beginning by following the slowly rising Plot Planner line. Anticipate the shift or reversal outside the character that sends her into the heart of the story world. Plot it.

Plotting the middle proves increasingly difficult as you're forced to throw all sorts of horrible people and situations at your protagonist. Pace the intensity of these scenes as they reflect his changing emotional development and foreshadow the coming disaster. Look to the Plot Planner for ideas on how to convey the character's emotional reaction to the challenges that confront him. Search the notes you made about the character emotional development on the Plot Planner to spot patterns in his behavior. Does he always run when the going gets tough? Does he turn belligerent when under pressure? Does he accuse and blame others for his misfortunes? Introducing his character reactions in the beginning of the story allows you to incrementally deepen the reader's understanding of how that repetitive pattern affects him emotionally in the middle. In the end, you have the opportunity to show the character acting and reacting in entirely new ways, incorporating all he's learned and overcome.

By focusing on what is interfering with her success, the protagonist is controlled by problems. Let those problems take her where they want her to go. Keep her off balance and her emotions soaring. She should give the antagonistic elements and people in her life strength, feed their growth, and lessen her own. Anticipate the crisis, the next scene of highest intensity in the story so far, and the lowest point for the protagonist as she is forced to awaken to the bigger problem, villain, stakes, need, or challenge. Write what causes her to become conscious of a shift or reversal inside her, and place it on the Plot Planner line.

In the end, the protagonist has learned to focus on potential solutions rather than his problems. He takes control and begins leading his life in the direction he wants it to go. This change of perspective at the end sets up the climax where, in scene, he demonstrates being fully united with his new self-knowledge, new understanding of the world, and new sense of responsibility through his actions and his words.

Plotting out the protagonist's emotional development on the Plot Planner gives you a visual representation of her transformation. Comparing how the character develops later in the story to how she handled situations earlier in the story allows you to better control your pacing. You can decide when to pull back in reflective scenes and when to charge ahead with pressure scenes. The Plot Planner guides your pacing scene by scene.

At the same time, with your notes in place for the dramatic action and the character emotional development, the Plot Planner allows you to see the different plot threads and their interplay throughout your story. By plotting the scenes above or below the line, and indicating the two plotline elements in two different colors, you are able to see the ebb and flow of all your scenes at once.

KEEPING THE CHARACTER CONSISTENT

Character consistency is essential to keeping your readers deeply rooted in your story world. If the protagonist acts "out of character" or does something counter to the personality you've established, without some sort of foreshadowing or development, the reader feels cheated. You can avoid confusing your readers and cluttering your imagination by plotting a logical progression toward a breakdown along the middle of your plot planner, as well as the steps to his build-up at the end. Stand back from the words and gain access to a larger context as you allow him to emerge and develop with a better understanding of the significance of each of the story parts.

If you are developing a character like Novalee, who has difficulty asking for help in the beginning of *Where the Heart Is*, check your sticky notes on the Plot Planner for each interaction she has with others. Be on the lookout for any instance where she falls out of "character" by suddenly speaking up for herself. If she speaks up for herself in one instance, the reader will wonder why she can't do it in another. Too many character inconsistencies like that cause the reader to detach from the character.

If, however, the protagonist speaks up on another person's behalf, then you've deepened the reader's understanding of her flaw. By witnessing her ability to speak up for another, the reader is better able to assess just how disconnected the protagonist is from herself.

INSERTING FORESHADOWING

We've discussed how to link scenes by cause and effect, and how each event leads to the next, moment by moment and scene by scene. Foreshadowing links scenes from the present to scenes that will happen in the future. Anytime you leave clues or allude to something mysterious, ominous, uncertain, or potentially life changing that will occur in the future, you are using foreshadowing. Always be on the lookout for ways to foreshadow seemingly insignificant events, objects, locations, character traits, reactions, and actions that will eventually take on significance later in the story.

Before you can layer your scenes with foreshadowing, a sense of the larger story is necessary. You first need to determine where all the different elements rest and all the different character clues hide. Professional writers don't reveal everything that is coming up front. Instead they leave hints.

The reader (and the protagonist) doesn't have an outline of the story and thus can only anticipate what is coming by discerning the clues given along the way by the use of foreshadowing. The life of the story takes on its own shape, and its sequence seems inevitable to the reader and audience because of foreshadowing.

The middle challenges the protagonist in an unfamiliar territory. Throughout all the setbacks and obstacles, the middle also provides the protagonist with opportunities to learn, discover, or rediscover a gift, clue, belief, ability, or skill that serves her in her final confrontation at the end. The act of discovery is often used as an act of foreshadowing in stories.

TIPS FOR USING FORESHADOWING IN THE MIDDLE

- Decide what skills, abilities, beliefs, knowledge and wisdom, tricks, clues, behaviors and mannerisms, talents, and powers the protagonist needs to succeed at the climax.
- Decide which of these lessons she'll *need* at the end and which ones she will be *without* in the beginning and the middle. Separate each lesson into one of these categories:

    - She is unaware of this particular gift or talent.
    - She never learned this particular lesson.
    - She needs to learn this lesson in the second half of the middle.

- Decide who is going to teach her what she needs to learn and how to integrate that into the plot without giving away the importance of the skill.
- Have the lessons the protagonist learns come out of the external events of the middle and be directly tied to one or more of the characters in the middle as part of their shared subplots.
- Neither the characters nor the reader should know the lesson's significance to the end. The reader should be engaged with the dramatic action of the middle, and whatever skills and abilities the protagonist learns should be on the sidelines, secondary to the main action, and *not the protagonist's intended goal* in the scene. For instance, the protagonist's goal in a scene should not be to learn how to pick a lock. Instead she should learn to pick a lock because of what's happening in the story. Later, in the final quarter of the story, she discovers how valuable this skill is when she must use it to save herself and save the day.
- Attempt to make the lessons learned part of the front story and keep the protagonist from using the new skill until it appears that all is lost at the climax.
- Sometimes the foreshadowing that appears in the middle is portrayed as the protagonist teaching another character (and the reader) something he needs to understand in order to uncover clues and solve the mystery at the end.

Chapter Thirteen

PLOT THE THEMATIC SIGNIFIGANCE

Months after readers have finished a great story, many cannot recall the action in scenes or describe the character development. However, even years later, those same readers still hold an idea, if vague, of what the story was about. They remember the underlying theme. As important as dramatic action and character emotional development are to a story, the reader wants all the action in all the scenes to add up to something significant and meaningful. This chapter addresses thematic significance and how to develop meaning in your plot.

Theme is what your story is about as an *abstraction* beyond the action. It is an *idea* that your story proposes or supposes, a speculated truth. Every story speculates on a possible truth (theme). Often the thematic significance of your story can be found in the change the characters undergo as a result of the core conflict in the story.

FINDING THE THEMATIC SIGNIFICANCE OF YOUR STORY

The following questions can help you find the theme of your story:

- What message do you want the reader to be left with after she has finished reading your book?
- Why are you writing the book?

- What are you trying to say?
- What is the overall conclusion you want your readers to walk away with?

Do not worry if you are unable to answer these questions until after you have written a draft or two—theme is most resonant when it is not imposed on the story but comes from within it. If you have not yet discovered the theme of your project, write down the questions above and tape the list to your computer. Then keep searching as you write.

Eventually you do want to know the theme for two reasons:

1. Theme matters to the reader. Readers today are deluged with books and magazines and the Internet. For them to commit their precious time to reading your story, you must provide a deeper message beyond the pure enjoyment of reading your words. Theme defines what is at stake in your story.
2. The more clearly you can define your theme, the tighter your story. Once you know your theme, your scene choices will follow theme, as opposed to following other possibilities.

Your theme anchors you to your subject.

⊂▭▭▭▷ PLOT THE THEMATIC SIGNIFICANCE

Once you know your theme, you can review your plotline and mark the scenes that demonstrate the theme. Trust the process; all the answers you need are in your story right now. It's up to you to find them. Your theme serves as a compass on your journey, determining where you are currently on course in what you have written and where you have stumbled down a dead-end or veered off the trail.

You should be able to sum up your theme in a thematic significance statement. Here are a few examples of what this statement looks like:

> "A person's truest nature, who they truly are, can't be killed off and must be rediscovered to achieve true happiness."

"By accepting both good and the evil, strength and weakness, love and hate, beauty and ugliness as inseparable and codependent, you can give birth to creativity."

"Family loyalty leads to a life of crime."

Once you know your theme, write it out in sentence form as a thematic significance statement. This is what your story is attempting to prove. Write this sentence across the top of your Plot Planner as a reminder to incorporate the theme into every scene by way of your use of details, in every choice and decision the character makes, and within the character's emotional development.

Explore the sticky notes on your Plot Planner for signs of the prevalent themes your story deals with. Look for common themes in the action and in the character's emotional development. Wherever you find metaphors or reoccurring symbols, note ideas about how to highlight the meaning in the details to best lead the reader to the conclusion you're developing thematically.

DERIVING THEME FROM WITHIN

One way or another, you will prove something to your readers through your story.

In our writing, we authors usually focus on topics we care deeply about, are interested in exploring, are grappling with in our own lives, or simply find fascinating. Oftentimes themes for our stories originate from our own past. Stick a note in a distinct color on your Plot Planner where similar thematic topics are addressed in your scenes. Look for images or experiences that mirror those in your life and that have remained distinct through the passage of time. The big traumatic moments pop right to the surface. Stay still and wait awhile. The next image to surface may surprise you. Buried in those experiences are beliefs by which you have lived your life. Likely they'll show up in your stories. Find the scenes where they pop up and indicate on your Plot Planner various ways to develop these themes.

The following are some examples of how themes can manifest from our own experiences.

Example 1

One of my students remembers being chastised in front of her entire class in an early grade for challenging the teacher's words. Although she was ultimately proven right, the student never forgot the humiliation she suffered. With that one memory she discovered she had been living her life and writing her stories with the belief that speaking up, speaking out, and speaking back comes at a price.

Example 2

An artist paints a picture of a garden. The colors, shading, and composition of the piece are flawless and deserve attention. Another artist has a deep emotional wound from her past that has left her with the belief that people are "no damn good." She paints the same garden, but she integrates into the composition a pair of scissors.

Example 3

A single mother with children to feed is grateful to land a job as a night security guard.

Once on the job, the woman hears screams and pleading coming from the warehouse on the property. The boss is abusing the workers with a cattle prod. Workers beg for mercy as they are held against their will.

The boss instructs the woman to throw the switch to the electrical fence if any of the workers tries to escape over the barbed wire. Then the boss leaves.

Until this point, the woman has shown disbelief on her face and discomfort in her body language, but, even so, she does as she is told. The character must make a decision when the workers plead for mercy as they try to escape.

The following are three different reactions to the same experience based on three different life experiences.

1. If you've learned that in order to keep your job, you do what you are told, no matter how inhumane you believe it is, you will throw the switch.
2. If you've learned that when someone is down, he should be kicked, you might not only throw the switch but may also trip the workers as they attempt to escape.
3. If you've learned that there comes a time in everyone's life when you have to take a stand, you will refuse to throw the switch and instead will quit your job.

For each scenario, your life experiences have a direct influence on your choices and decisions and shape your individual themes.

No matter what we write, the process is an exploration of ourselves. Our own beliefs and themes pop up when we least expect it. Sometimes we discover that what we thought were our beliefs do not translate onto the page, and so we must delve even deeper to find out what it is we truly believe.

If your characters display a mind of their own and deviate from the plot you envisioned for them, ask yourself if the resistance is coming from your inner self. Your deeper self may be begging for the opportunity to come into the light and force you to confront your real truth: not the truth you were brought up to believe, and not the truth of the world around you, but your own authentic truth.

By your final draft, you have an idea of the deeper meaning of your story, what you are trying to say, and the ways you have attempted to communicate that meaning through your story to your audience.

When the dramatic action changes the character emotional development at depth over time, the story becomes thematically significant.

THE STORY CONCEPT

Not only does thematic significance bring meaning and coherence to your story, it also helps you form your story concept. Let's say you attend a writers conference and find yourself sitting next to a literary agent at lunch. How quickly and compellingly can you draw her into your story? The answer is determined by how intriguing your concept is.

Rather than drone on about every plot point, learn how to rattle off a pithy pitch that entices your listener and has her begging you for more. Think of the concept and pitch as the seeds of action and characters interacting in a meaningful way.

Some writers won't write a word until they come up with a concept that contains a certain "snap," a uniqueness based on a universal truth, something special, exotic, or unexpected. Others don't tackle the task until they've finished writing and editing, and are ready to query.

Wherever you are with your story, the time is never too early to ask yourself: What is your story *about*? Brainstorm concepts that fit your story. The more unique and unusual and original, the better. Stretch, think big, and think differently to hook someone with your concept. Without a compelling concept, a story may never find an agent, a publisher, or an audience. Keep a notebook of ideas, and narrow down what your story is about to one or two lines.

Intrigue, mystery, romance, secrets and lies, wrongful arrest and sentencing, betrayal, and loyalty are all provocative plot points that can manifest into themes within a high-concept story.

The following are two methods for creating a winning concept.

1. The "Who Wants What and Why, and What's Stopping Her?" Concept

> *Sand and Secrets* is a mystery told from alternating points of view about the descendants of a cigar dynasty. Sarah, a Cuban prostitute with a fetish for cigars, and Nick, a high-rolling American gambler, must be the first to find the breach in the cigar distribution system or lose their chance at inheriting the family business.

This short paragraph says enough to create intrigue, and it includes all three plotlines.

The dramatic action plot centers on the dramatic question: Will the security breach be found in time to save the company? Who will find it first?

The character emotional development plot centers on Sarah, a prostitute with a fetish for cigars, and Nick, a high-rolling American gambler.

At this point, the story hinges more on the quirky characterizations of the point-of-view characters and less on a higher thematic calling. If one of them has a goal of solving the mystery that includes a higher purpose, this is the thematic significance.

As the concept is written here, the intrigue of the tale is enough for agents, editors, and readers to ask for more and thus satisfy the basic demand of a story concept.

2. The X+Y+Z Concept

X (your main character or protagonist) is in Y (the general place, time, and circumstances of the protagonist's everyday life when the novel begins) until Z (the catalyst that makes the story a story occurs).

> Joleen, a sixteen-year-old single mother of triplets [X], leads a dead-end life in a thug-infested neighborhood where her unique ability has been forgotten [Y], until one of the warring gangs blows up her home, forcing her into action to protect her kids [Z].

EXAMPLES OF THEME

Themes are the fundamental and often universal ideas explored in fiction. Here are some examples of theme statements from classic literature. See if you agree with the statements, or come up with your own. Consider which statements convey the essence of the story.

- "Things are not always what they appear." (*To Kill a Mockingbird* by Harper Lee)
- "A spiritual journey is challenging but, when undertaken with passion and dedication, can transform a person enough to overcome hurt, and love again." (*Eat Pray Love* by Elizabeth Gilbert)

- "Fascination with wealth is self-destructive." (*The Great Gatsby* by F. Scott Fitzgerald)
- "Beneath the surface of seemingly ordinary women lay extraordinary lives." (*The Stone Diaries* by Carol Shields)
- "When a boy is coming of age and the only life he has ever known is disappearing into the past, in order to claim his place in the world, that boy must leave on a dangerous and harrowing journey. (*All the Pretty Horses* by Cormac McCarthy)
- "Through ambition and courage, man is able to survive against all odds." (*The Sea-Wolf* by Jack London)
- "To find a place for oneself, one must first break away." (*White Oleander* by Janet Fitch)
- "Home is where the heart is." (*Where the Heart Is* by Billie Letts)
- "Man has a collective tendency to go overboard toward generosity and forgiveness." (*The Adventures of Tom Sawyer* by Mark Twain)
- "Man cannot escape his destiny but may be ennobled in the attempt." (*Oedipus Rex* by Sophocles)
- "Family loyalty leads to a life of crime." (*The Godfather* by Mario Puzo)
- "Forgiveness of others begins with forgiveness of the self. (*Love Made of Heart* by Teresa LeYung Ryan)
- "Courage leads to redemption." (*The Old Man and the Sea* by Ernest Hemingway)
- "Forced self-examination leads to generosity." (*A Christmas Carol* by Charles Dickens)
- "The human spirit can withstand even the most ruthless circumstances." (*One Flew Over the Cuckoo's Nest* by Ken Kesey)
- "When left to their own devices, people naturally revert to cruelty, savagery, and barbarism." (*Lord of the Flies* by William Golding)
- "Affection, loyalty, and conscience are more important than social advancement, wealth, and class." (*Great Expectations* by Charles Dickens)

- "Independent ideas cannot always translate into a simultaneously self-sufficient and socially acceptable existence." (*The Awakening* by Kate Chopin)
- "Patterns of inequality in human rights based on racial differences are unjust and ultimately intolerable." (*Cry, the Beloved Country* by Alan Paton)
- "A person who learns the profound effect he has had on his family and community is given a renewed faith to live." (*It's a Wonderful Life*; story written by Philip Van Doren Stern and movie directed by Frank Capra)
- "A tight-knit family, no matter how poor, can survive anything." (*Grapes of Wrath* by John Steinbeck)
- "Being different is a secret that all humans share." (*Stones from the River* by Ursula Hegi)
- "Friends can fill an empty heart." (*Because of Winn-Dixie* by Kate DiCamillo)
- "The will to survive can bring material success; yet paired with narcissism and a lack of compassion, it will lead to loss of love." (*Gone with the Wind* by Margaret Mitchell)

The thematic significance statement communicates what all of the scenes and dramatic action together add up to mean in the end. Create a thematic significance statement that encompasses the emotional transformation your protagonist undergoes from the beginning to the end of the story.

MORE ON THEME

A visual representation of the theme of your story emerges as you view your Plot Planner and ponder the meaning behind specific scenes. Note how the different plot threads interplay throughout the story; which scenes are above or below the line; how the three plotlines rise and fall together, each in a different color; and how the scenes ebb and flow at the overall story level.

Holding up your scenes and characters against a backdrop of the whole story gives you fuller access to a larger context of meaning. An entire world emerges, along with a better understanding of the significance of each of its parts.

As you evaluate each part of your story for theme at the overall story level, you will need to decide how to handle thematic details in the beginning, middle, and end. For example, you might discover that your story's core explores the risks your protagonist is willing to take for the one she loves. Look for how you introduce the concepts of both love and of risk taking in the beginning. In the middle, deepen the reader's understanding of risk taking and love in all the various forms of theme you wish to portray.

One way to do this is to include a character in the story who embodies the opposite traits of your protagonist; perhaps he is overly cautious and unwilling to open up, commit, or go out on a limb for anyone. Reveal the positive effects of using caution in a relationship(s), thereby seemingly disproving the theme. When your protagonist, who believes risk taking is necessary to be with the one you love, interacts with someone who challenges her belief system, it creates tension.

To deepen the theme in the middle section, consider how the conflicts and challenges your protagonist suffers at the hand of the antagonists affect her ideas of risk taking and love as she moves steadily (so she hopes) toward her goal. Does the middle of your story deepen the reader's understanding of all aspects of the thematic significance?

Show what safety and caution in dating look and feel like. Let us feel her emotion—don't just tell us about how she feels. Show the reader how her confusion, doubt, and uncertainty reveal itself through her actions, dialogue, attitude, posture, and habits.

When characters who embody the ideal of what or who the protagonist is trying to be, or reveal an unexpected shadow side that the protagonist has failed to consider, another facet of the theme is presented.

In the final quarter of the story, the protagonist emerges from the middle into the territory of the end. There the primary role of the dramatic action is to get the protagonist to the right place at the right time for the final confrontation while also demonstrating how different the character's actions and reactions are compared to the beginning of the story. In rapid succession, do your scenes build in significance and relevance as the protagonist makes choices about what she is willing to do for love? Tension, conflict, and suspense rise until the character emotional development and the dramatic action plotlines collide head-on at the climax.

After the peak energy at the climax settles, we learn whether the protagonist has been deeply changed or not. This is where the thematic significance plotline is at its most meaningful. A character fighting to gain what he desires is capable of producing an outcome of important consequence. With illumination, insight, or a tiny bit of wisdom, the story promise you made to your readers at the beginning of the book is kept.

Chapter Fourteen

WHEN TO PLOT

I invite you to use the Plot Planner in any way you find the most useful to your writing life. The following are three points in your writing where you might find it most valuable to use these forms.

I recommend that you plot out your story at least three times during a writing project:

1. **PRE-PLOT:** before you begin writing your project
2. **REVISION:** after you have completed a first draft
3. **FINAL EDIT:** before you call your project "final"

1. PRE-PLOT

There seem to be two general categories of writers: those who do not pre-plot their writing projects, and those who do.

Writers who do not pre-plot are often referred to as intuitive writers. They prefer to work things out on the page. The other group of writers finds that making things up as they go with no advance planning is like skydiving without a parachute. Since the objective of this book is to support you in your writing, do what works for you.

Long before we begin writing, each of us has some idea of what we want to say and why. Think of pre-plotting as a useful boundary that eliminates distractions that might lead you astray in your writing or take you on a wild-goose chase down blind alleys.

The muse often feeds us images in the same way that dreams do: ones that are disjointed, symbolic, and metaphoric. A Plot Planner is a form into which the muse can pour the vision. Once you create a plot structure, then you are free to imagine anything you want within those parameters. Or, as Wayne Muller writes in his book *Sabbath*, "... Imagine that certain limitations on our choices are actually seeds of great freedom."

A pre-plot is the place to put your ideas in some sort of order as you brainstorm, allowing the ideas to flow.

Granted this pre-plot you create will be merely a skeleton. You need not adhere too fervently to it. If you find you are pushing your characters around to fit into the grand design, and they are digging in their heels in in response, stop. Surrender to the characters' whims, and see what happens next. Either way, before you devote months, or possibly years, to a writing project, consider that the more pre-planning and careful thought you give, the less time you will spend rewriting.

2. REVISION

When you are ready to undertake a revision, it means you have arrived at a most important destination: completion of your first draft. Celebrate! The first draft is a test of faith and perseverance, and is a rite of passage for many writers.

The first draft separates those who write from those who just talk about writing.

Once the celebration is over, and before you start your first rewrite, (yes, there will be many more than one rewrite), reread your story to see what you have on the page. Then, rather than just going back through your piece, moving words around, and calling it a rewrite, I invite both the intuitive writers and the plotters both to take the time to carefully re-plot your story. There is no better way to analyze your project than to do a complete re-plot based on what you have written. The process alone gives you a new vision or sense of the structure of your project so you know what to hone, refine, and focus on in the rewrite.

Now stand back from your Plot Planner. With the experience of having written the climax scene at the end, you spot a plot that is now dangling and forgotten in the middle. The end reveals a random coincidence rather than a planned and thematically true event that leads the protagonist to the climax. Like weaving a textile, if one stitch is dropped, a hole begins to form. A weaver has to rip out the threads until she reaches the hole and then she re-weaves. You have the benefit as a writer to go back and weave in the dropped or underdeveloped threads.

As you re-plot your story, look for openings where you can broaden and intensify the more subtle implications of your original insight. Look for ways to exploit your scenes by making them carry as much weight as they can bear. Make sure the scenes are working for the story on all levels—character, action, theme, and, where appropriate, historical and political significance. Does the reader always know the who, what, where, and when of the scene? Have you incorporated "showing" details? Is there tension and conflict? Do the characters experience emotional change in every scene? Are the scenes well written?

As you re-examine the placement and pacing of your scenes, you may find some of them are static and, contrary to the visual sticky notes on your Plot Planner, may even decline in energy compared to the scenes that came before. Be careful not to be lulled by the Plot Planner, with its nicely rising lines, or it might trick you into believing your pacing and intensity match the ideal as represented by the rising Plot Planner line. Be thoughtful when you evaluate each scene for its level of tension or conflict. Then tweak your scenes by rearranging the order, deleting static scenes, or ramping up the tension so your story is truer to the ideal plot pattern.

At this point, a unifying premise or central theme might reveal itself. Some of us require the input of a few select, trusted readers to uncover the thread. Whatever it takes to find it, that thread will be invaluable as you rewrite.

3. FINAL EDIT

At this point, exhaustion has likely stepped in, and you might be tempted to proclaim to all your patient and loyal family and friends that you are finally finished. Please do not shoot the messenger, but I would like to recommend that you first take a deep breath and do a final plotting of your story before you make the heady declaration.

This is the time to test your final product:

- Examine every detail, every word, every sentence, and every connection.
- Is every summary relevant to the action that follows?
- Does every detail contribute to the thematic significance and make the dramatic action and the character emotional development more believable?
- Is every action meaningful?
- Does every scene contribute to the whole?
- Is the conflict rising slowly as it should?
- Have you provided adequate suspense?
- Is your core conflict resolved?
- Have you seamlessly integrated your theme throughout the project?
- Is the story fulfilled?

Are you sure? Okay, then go for it. Shout it from the highest hill! You're finished! Congratulations!

part two
SCENE TRACKER

TRACK THE SEVEN ESSENTIAL ELEMENTS OF SCENE

At its best, every scene in a story advances the dramatic action, develops the character, contributes to the theme, provides tension and conflict, and reflects a change in the character's attitude or circumstances. In short, *scenes* are at the core structure of a story.

In my plot-intensive workshops, it quickly becomes apparent that many writers are as confused about scene as they are about plot. Many writers think they are writing a scene when in fact they are writing a summary, telling readers what happens rather than showing. When they do show what's happening through action, dialogue, and details, their scenes have no true beginning, middle, or end—the basic core structure of scene, which mimics that of an overall plot. Or their scenes only complete one essential task, when each scene is capable of accomplishing a multitude of tasks. Due to confusion, most writers are not making the most of scene for the greater good of the story.

Scenes make plot. When I became determined to unravel the mysteries of plot, I knew I needed to address scene at the basic level.

THE SCENE TRACKER

Whether you are a screenwriter, a memoirist, or a writer of children's, young adult, or adult fiction, you write countless scenes. How does one make the most of all these scenes and keep track of all the information within the scenes? One simple technique is to create a visual representation of your story called a Scene Tracker. This is where you'll track all the most essential elements of plot in scenes. In doing so, you discover exactly where your strengths and weaknesses lie regarding scene writing. The Scene Tracker also works well for sorting out all the threads of your project, thereby saving you both time and effort.

The Scene Tracker is a grid that helps you track, scene by scene, all the dates and settings of the story, the character's emotional development and goals, the dramatic action, conflict, and the thematic significance, so that the whole does not become a tangled mess. Think of the Scene Tracker as the loom that holds your story ideas, scene fragments, character development, snippets of dialogue, research and details, and tension and conflict in roughly the order you envision the story will unfold. It helps you interweave all the threads for a successful narrative. When you start out, you may have lots of holes and gaps in your Scene Tracker, but these will be filled in as you come to know your story and characters better.

LAYOUT

You can build your Scene Tracker on:

- banner paper
- 11" × 17" sheets of paper
- a dry erase board
- your computer

I like to create my Scene Trackers on pieces of banner paper so I can hang them on the wall beside my computer screen. This way, my scene information is fully visible at all times. When inspiration strikes, I slap a sticky note on the Scene Tracker rather than filing it in a folder in a file cabinet or on my computer.

If you do not have the space to hang something as large as a piece of banner paper, or if you are not inclined to wallpaper your rooms with your scene information, try a smaller piece of paper or work on your computer. If you travel a great deal and want your story information readily available to you, consider purchasing a Scene Tracker Template at marthaalderson.com/scene-tracker-template.

Using the computer to create a Scene Tracker is not as effective for me as using a big piece of banner paper because the scene information is not as handy and visible. But it's important to choose the method that works best for you. If you choose to use your computer, just make sure that you print out your Scene Tracker so that it is readily available.

If you have already written a draft or two, the Scene Tracker will help with your rewrites. Use it to determine whether scenes and transitions, characters' emotional changes, and your use of detail are contributing to the fullest in the project's development.

This process may appear daunting or tedious to you. If so, start by tracking a few scenes to get a sense of your strengths and weaknesses in developing scene. Tackle the big, turning-point scenes first. Then, once you have tried out the system and have developed an understanding of what is important within a scene, track by chapters rather than by scenes.

You can also track only the sections of your story that appear weak to you so that you gain a better understanding of what might be missing or awaiting further development. Or you can simply track the scenes that lead up to the important turning points of your project, such as the crisis and/or the climax of your book. Keep in mind that the Scene Tracker is a system intended to help you with *your* writing by layering and deepening your scenes. Find a method that works best for you, and use it.

As one student of mine declared: "Using the Scene Tracker is like learning a new language or entering an alien culture. Many writers just think that they need to let the muse move them in any direction. Using the Scene Tracker, for me, involved adopting a new perspective on what I have written, and that was an anxiety-producing proposition." This same writer persevered. Like her, you can take a deep breath and persevere, and your writing life will never be the same.

In Part Two of *Writing Blockbuster Plots*, each of the seven essential elements that make up the Scene Tracker is given independent consideration. The examples provided show how successful writers integrated each of these aspects into a total structure to achieve unity.

FORMAT

Chapters fifteen and sixteen explain how to create a Scene Tracker. Chapters seventeen through twenty-four offer specific examples from published works for each step in the development of a Scene Tracker.

Using the same definition of plot we used earlier, notice the significance of scene in the overall definition of plot.

> Plot is a series of *scenes* arranged by cause and effect to create dramatic action filled with tension and conflict to further the character emotional development and provide thematic significance.

Except for the all-important scene, we have covered most of the elements mentioned in our definition of plot in the Plot Planner section of this book. In Part One, you generated shorthand sticky notes for the dramatic action, the character emotional development, and thematic significance for scenes you had written or imagined, and plotted them on your Plot Planner. Now it's time to investigate how plot is playing out at the scene level by evaluating each scene for seven essential elements.

You may choose to do this work directly on your Plot Planner using different-colored sticky notes for the different plotlines and scene elements. Let me caution you—that method can quickly overburden and clutter the Planner, leading to confusion rather than clarity. Instead I suggest using the Plot Planner for a broad view of your overall story and evaluating individual scenes for essential elements on a separate Scene Tracker.

Scene is where the story plays out and action ensues moment by moment. Each scene covers a relatively short period of time but is written in detail. Scene is focused motion with tension and conflict, and is built on talk and action, and experienced by both the character and the reader. A confrontation, a turning point, or a crisis occurs at given moments that take on significance and cannot be effectively summarized. Not all scenes contain earth-shattering events, but every scene has several layers of information packed into the moment. If you can convince readers to trust you by providing enticing character introductions and exciting action up front, they will believe you when you present the big action scenes to come.

Scene Tracker: *Candle in the Window* by Christina Dodd

SCENE (SC) OR SUMMARY (SU)	TIME AND SETTING	CHARACTER EMOTIONAL DEVELOPMENT	GOAL	DRAMATIC ACTION	CONFLICT		CHANGE IN EMOTION	THEMATIC DETAILS
The Beginning								
Ch. 5 Pg. 117 END OF THE BEGINNING	1153 Kidnapped	S. lies/explores W. W. faked being asleep	To make love	First X makes love W. can see again	+ / - / ++		S. questions whether she could live without W.	
The Middle								
Ch. 17, SC 2 and 3 CRISIS	Late summer Wedding guests have gone	Afraid W. won't believe her Ladies hadn't believed her Disappointed S. didn't trust him Asks only for a chance for S. to trust him	Figure things out Touch oak tree	Makes love, then works things out alone	X	- / -- / ---		Issues of S. lack of trust out in the open Her lack of trust in dog/self leads to kidnapping
The End								

Ch. 20, SC 2 and 4 CLIMAX	Prisoner in hole Darkness	Overcome by fear Unable to see again Opens up W. forced her to face herself Demonstrates her trust to climb cliff	To escape hole To prove her love	Escape hole and climb sheer cliff	X	+ / - / ++	Trust resolved
RESOLU-TION							

SCENE IDENTIFICATION

Take out the piece of writing you have chosen to work with, preferably your own. Next, close your eyes and take a couple of deep breaths. Relax. Concentrate on your breathing. There is no right or wrong in what I am offering here. These are ideas that have helped other writers, and I offer them to you so that you do not have to go it alone.

Go through the piece of writing you are working on and, page by page, mark where you believe each scene begins and ends.

Does this brief exercise reveal your confusion about the difference between a scene and a summary? If so, refer to chapter fifteen for explanations and examples of scene and summary. If you are confident about your ability to identify scene versus summary, bypass chapter fifteen altogether and move directly to creating a Scene Tracker in chapter sixteen.

If you enjoy multitasking, use a different-colored marker to mark the summaries at the same time you identify scenes. Though scenes often begin with a short summary, look for where action begins and mark the scene beginning there.

Next, read for the following, and mark the end of these scenes:

- a cliff-hanger
- a disaster
- a decision
- a change in location

Do not make a list of the scenes and summaries. Mark the beginnings and endings directly on your manuscript.

Scenes show outward action. They are in the now, unfolding moment by moment. Dialogue is a scene marker and action is, too.

TAKE A BREAK

Get up and make yourself a cup of tea. Now sit back and look over your manuscript. Is there a pattern made visible in the markings? Take a deep breath. Invite in the spirit of discovery. See your story in a new way.

Chapter Fifteen

SCENE VERSUS SUMMARY

A great scene invites readers to immerse themselves in a story, absorb the words, and become the character. They aren't stopping to think about what's happening but are living in the scene and viscerally processing each moment. The following scene is a terrific example.

> Charlie felt the hot rush of shot fly past his face, and his legs shook under him with the boom of the gun. But it was a clean miss, and he started to run at Jerry, closing the distance even as Jerry fished in his pocket for another load. Twenty feet …
>
> Jerry cursed and broke open the breech. Twelve feet …
> He slapped in the fresh shell. Eight feet …
> He snapped the gun closed. Six feet …
> He threw it to his shoulder. Four feet …
> He saw a fist the size of a lard bucket come flying at his nose.

This is a scene from *Ava's Man* by Rick Bragg. The confrontation between Charlie and Jerry is of intense importance to the memoir and is being played out moment by moment on the page. Jerry has a goal to shoot Charlie before he gets close enough to harm him. The immediate conflict comes in the form of the fist flying at Jerry's head. Both of these details lead to a sense of impending disaster. The action in the scene is exciting. The reader's eyes speed across the page as every step is broken down. Time slows, allowing the reader to slip into the scene.

The reader feels every breath, hears the ticking of time, and cringes. Which will come first—the gunshot or the fist? Will Jerry succeed?

Tension. Conflict. This is page-turning excitement unfolded in slow motion through action, told in scene.

When you gain an appreciation for the core structure of a scene, you are able to exploit the scenes for the greater good of the story. There is another added plus: If you understand scene, the plot naturally follows.

Charlie's family may have come out on the porch to see what all the commotion was about, or there might have been traffic on the road behind them, but all that matters to this scene is what is happening between these two men. Because it is so well written, no dialogue is necessary.

You will probably write many scenes that end up in the recycling bin. This does not mean the scenes were not important to write. Often it is in the process of writing a scene that we discover important information about our characters, but that does not always mean that this is information the reader needs to know. A good writer knows which scenes to keep, which scenes to combine, and which scenes to cut. The Scene Tracker will help you determine which is which.

Be careful—once you show something in scene, do not follow up with a summary to underline a point. Trust your showing abilities, and trust your readers.

WHAT IS A SCENE? WHAT IS SUMMARY?

You have likely heard the writer's mantra "Show, don't tell." A scene *shows*. Summary *tells*.

Each scene has a tiny plot structure of its own, beginning with steps taken toward a goal or desire, followed by some sort of conflict and tension, and ending with failure, an unanswered question, or a cliff-hanger—something that entices the reader to continue reading.

All conflict, confrontations, and turning points—the high points of your story—must be played out in scene on the page, in real time.

In creating a Scene Tracker for your individual story, you will need to differentiate between a scene and a summary. We're not as concerned about whether the character is taking action with a goal in mind or reacting to a disaster, but only that action is acted out in a scene rather than told in summary.

Scene is core to story, and this is where we will spend most of our time. But not every moment can be conveyed in scene. This is where summary comes into play. By condensing the parts of time that are not interesting or pivotal to the plot, summary moves your story quickly from one important event and through the seconds or minutes or years that pass before the next important event. This allows you to show time periods in a plot flashing by in a short sentence or spanning centuries in a paragraph.

"To write simply is as difficult as to be good." –W. Somerset Maugham

SUMMARY

Story is conflict shown in scene. Yet a story made up entirely of scenes can inject too much conflict and become exhausting for the reader. A summary is a place to rest. Instead of playing out every moment on the page in scene, you can use summary to compress time when appropriate.

Summary narrates quickly those events that are not important enough to the overall storyline to *show* in detail. Summary relates those events in their sequence but compresses them or *tells* how things were during a particular period of time. The use of summary is helpful in moving quickly, so that you can focus on creating scenes to *show* the moments that are the most important to your plot.

Use summary to:

• provide information
• fill in a character's backstory
• set up the next action
• tell the general circumstances

- show motive
- change the pace
- create a transition
- move quickly through time

In one of my workshops, a historical fiction writer expressed concern that her story was too long. Using the Scene Tracker, she immediately spotted the problem: She had told her story entirely in scene. Historical fiction is generally longer and broader in scope than most contemporary fiction, and so the use of summary becomes critical.

There are two types of summary you can employ in your work.

Circumstantial Summary

Circumstantial summary sums up the circumstances of the characters over a set period of story time.

> The days went by. The women and children moved eastward through rain and bitter cold that caused their clothes and blankets to freeze during the night. So difficult was the terrain, on some days they were able to progress less than three miles.

This is an example of circumstantial summary from *True Women* by Janet Woods Windle. The passage describes the general circumstances for these women and children—what these women's lives were like on the trail and the sorts of hardships they endured. Because summary is telling, it sets us apart from the action. However, in this case, the author works around that by using sensory details to infuse the summary with life and immediacy.

Sequential Summary

Sequential summary sums up the sequence of events for the characters over a set period of story time.

> Consider the case of the female black leopard that escaped from the Zurich zoo in the winter of 1933. She was new to the zoo and seemed to get along with the male leopard. But various paw injuries hinted at matrimonial strife. Before any decision could be taken about what to do, she squeezed

through a break in the roof bars of her cage and vanished in the night. The discovery that a wild carnivore was free in their midst created an uproar among the citizens of Zurich. Traps were set and hunting dogs were let loose. They only rid the canton of its few half-wild dogs. Not a trace of the leopard was found for ten weeks. Finally, a casual labourer came upon it under a barn twenty-five miles away and shot it.

This passage from *Life of Pi* by Yann Martel relates in a compressed sequence the important events that happened over a ten-week period. This is an example of sequential summary.

If you find yourself quickly summarizing events, stop and ask: Am I shying away from creating this scene because the material seems too hard, too long, or too painful to write? If the answer is yes, take a deep breath and write the events out moment by bloody moment. Perhaps start by writing a scene with dialogue only, or write in action snippets. You may find yourself crying, sweating, and swearing at the screen in front of you. Do not give up. Keep at it. Dig deep. Use the emotion.

Again, summary is important, but it is an explanation or *telling*. Scene is experiential. The more scenes you use, the more you are *showing* and the less you are *telling*. The key is to find a balance. The Scene Tracker helps you do that.

USING THE SCENE TRACKER FOR DETERMINING SCENE VS. SUMMARY

When a character thinks about something, this is considered a cerebral activity and is generally written in summary. If he is feeling something, this is considered visceral and is generally written in scene. (Keep in mind, a character thinking about how she feels is still thinking; thus it is cerebral and likely told in summary.)

Track your story. How much out-of-body or in-the-head time does your story encompass? How much in-the-body time?

Use the Scene Tracker to deepen each and every scene you write.

In Part One this book, we used the Plot Planner to show and discuss how plot works at the overall story level. We determined which scenes belong above the Plot Planner line and which ones belong below the line. Now we dig a step deeper by evaluating whether a passage is a scene or a summary.

Even if your story has exciting and meaningful action and features a strong, flawed character who is unafraid of taking big risks and is willing to show his dark side (which is my favorite kind of protagonist), if too many of the scenes fall below the Plot Planner line and the rest are written in summary, the story stalls. This same flaw quickly becomes evident on the Scene Tracker when you see summary after summary indicated rather than exciting action scenes. Summary creates distance, which is counterproductive to reader engagement.

But never fear: The potential for switching summary to above-the-line scenes is terrific so long as when you rewrite in the next draft, you focus on creating moment-by-moment conflict, tension, suspense, and/or curiosity that incites the dramatic question: Will or won't the character succeed? First-draft scenes generally grow in excitement in subsequent drafts as you add more essential elements: authentic and thematic details, greater emotion, deeper character development, and snappier action.

Summaries occupy a vital place in storytelling, especially when they create more intensity and depth with a pallor of tension, a hint of conflict, and a whisper of overarching suspense.

CREATE THE
SCENE TRACKER FORM

THE SEVEN ESSENTIAL ELEMENTS OF SCENE

The technique of slowing down the action in scenes forces the stakes in a story ever higher. At the same time, the stakes also rise for you the writer. Many beginning writers hide from the pressure of creating scenes by relying solely on summary and narration. These same writers hold the mistaken belief that *telling* what happens is a more controllable arena than *showing* in scene.

My contention is that if you break down scene into its smallest parts, you retain control.

Like plot, scene has many different layers and functions. The Scene Tracker addresses seven of these essential plot elements as shown in scene.

The seven functions of scene are as follows:

- Time and Setting
- Character Emotional Development
- Goal
- Dramatic Action
- Conflict
- Change in Emotion
- Thematic Details

Scenes can have plenty of other functions—minor character development, the villain's development, tracking the romance or the mystery, political undertones, environmental overtones, and the like—but as long as you truly see and understand each of the seven elements discussed and developed in Part Two of this book, you will be better equipped to develop not only those seven but also the others.

The more you understand each of the seven functions of scene, the more you will be able to deepen the meaning of your piece through nuance in subsequent rewrites. The more you can do that, the better you can fulfill your promise to the reader.

THE SCENE TRACKER AT WORK

As great as the Plot Planner and Scene Tracker templates are for creating blockbuster plots, they are also a terrific means to see how plot concepts work in classic and best-selling fiction. Let me show you what I mean with the following example from *The Adventures of Tom Sawyer* by Mark Twain. The theme of this story is: "Man has a collective tendency to go overboard toward generosity and forgiveness."

For now, I just want you to have a sense of what a Scene Tracker looks like: the plot elements (each one drawn from the plot definition we defined earlier), columns, and headers. We will go over this form step by step in the following chapters.

Scene Tracker: *The Adventures of Tom Sawyer* by Mark Twain							
SCENE (SC) OR SUMMARY (SU)	TIME AND SETTING	CHARACTER EMOTIONAL DEVELOPMENT	GOAL	DRAMATIC ACTION	CONFLICT	CHANGE IN EMOTION	THEMATIC DETAILS
Ch. 1, SC 1	Fri. Aunt's house	Tom: Small, smart, fast, prankster, liar Aunt: Softy; took in dead sister's son	Escape	Tom/Aunt trouble	X	-/-/+	Aunt quotes the Good Book: "Spare the rod and spoil the child."
Ch. 1, SU							
Ch. 1, SC 2	Fri. Dinner		Not to be found out/cut school	Interrogated	X (Will he or won't he be found out?)	+/-/+/-	

identify which scene you're tracking and where each scene falls in the overall sequence of your story presentation.

TIME AND SETTING COLUMN: This is where you indicate the passage of time within the scene and, when appropriate, historical dates and events that take place during that time frame. This is also where you will indicate the scene's setting.

CHARACTER EMOTIONAL DEVELOPMENT COLUMN: The character's emotional development represents the heart of your story and is one of the three major plotlines. This column is where you'll indicate what traits and background you introduce about the character in the beginning section, make shorthand comments about how you deepen the reader's appreciation of the character's emotional limitations in the middle, and jot down notes about how she demonstrates a change in her thinking, behavior, and/or emotions in the end.

GOAL COLUMN: The protagonist has a specific goal in every scene that he or she hopes to attain.

DRAMATIC ACTION COLUMN: This column represents the action in the story.

CONFLICT COLUMN: Story is conflict shown in scene. This is the column where you indicate if the action you list in the Dramatic Action Column is dramatic (marked with an *X*) or passive (indicated by no *X*).

CHANGE IN EMOTION COLUMN: Story is change. This is where you track the fleeting emotional changes the character moves through within each scene. A positive change is indicated by a "+" sign, while a negative change is indicated by a "-" sign.

THEMATIC DETAILS COLUMN: The theme is the why, the spirit of your story, your reason for writing the story, what you want your readers to take away from having read it. This column represents the border of your tapestry.

Ch. 1, SU				Whistling			
Ch. 1, SC 3	Fri. Evening	Not one to fight right away	Figure out new boy	Exchanges insults with new boy	X (Will he or won't he figure out the new boy?)	+/-/-	Aunt forgave him earlier. Will he forgive new boy?
Ch. 2, SC 4	Sat. morning, field	Hates work Intro: J	To get out of work	White-wash fence	X (Will he or won't he get out of work?)	-/-	Aunt fights her forgiving nature to punish Tom
SU				Painting			
Ch. 2, SC 5	Minutes later	Clever	Get someone else to do work	Ignores friend; friend falls for it	X (Will he or won't he get someone else to do the work?)	+/+	T.'s friends end up paying him to work

Note: Refer to Appendix III for an example of how these scenes plot out on a Plot Planner.

⟨▭▭▶ CREATE A SCENE TRACKER

To create a Scene Tracker, start by dividing a piece of paper into eight columns. I prefer to use a piece of banner paper that is about six feet long, but you can use whatever suits your individual needs.

Think of this form as the warp (using the weaving metaphor again), or foundation, of your story. For each column, note that the trick is to create a succinct, concise, pithy, and to-the-point description that represents the element covered in that particular column and embodied in that particular scene.

The Scene Tracker Columns

The first column of the Scene Tracker is where you indicate what chapter you are tracking, which scene you are working on, and, when appropriate, where your summaries appear. Each of the other seven columns represents one of the seven essential plot elements in every scene.

SCENE/SUMMARY COLUMN: This column represents the frame of your story and contains chapter and scene number information. It does not represent an essential element of plot. Rather this is the place to

TAKE A BREAK

Before we move on to filling in the Scene Tracker, sit back and look at the form of the Scene Tracker. The Scene Tracker is a visual aid in seeing the structure of your story and serves as a reminder that a story awaits you. Imagine where you will hang it.

When the Scene Tracker is filled in, you will see your story in ways that are not possible in simply reading what you have written. When the luster of words and phrases is removed, the Scene Tracker form is the representation of your expression. Just as it is difficult to see the forest for the trees, it is difficult to see the form of your story for the words. Mysteries and depth are hiding in your stories right now. It is on the Scene Tracker in the interlocking plotlines that they reveal themselves.

Hang your Scene Tracker vertically on the wall beside your computer screen so it is fully visible at all times. Or print out enough copies of the Scene Tracker template to cover the number of scenes in your story. Use one template sheet per chapter. Organize and group the sheets by the beginning, middle, and end of your story. Flip through them, and integrate and modify notations as you write and rewrite your scenes.

Do not track more than a few chapters of scenes in one sitting. Stop when you run out of inspiration.

When inspiration strikes again, make a note on the Tracker. Never again will you lose an idea, a reminder, a prompt, or a question because it was filed away in a folder in a file cabinet or on your computer.

When you are ready—and only then—move on in this book. Chapters seventeen through twenty-four provide straightforward explanations and examples of how other writers brilliantly layered their scenes.

Chapter Seventeen

THE SCENE OR SUMMARY COLUMN

In chapter fourteen, you marked the starting and stopping points of the scenes and summaries in your manuscript. The first column on the Scene Tracker is where you indicate the chapter and the scene number. By primarily tracking scenes, we emphasize their importance in carrying the full weight of the plot. We do not track summary on a scene tracker beyond noting "SU" when a summary appears between scenes. If, however, an important date is mentioned in a summary or a pivotal event is summarized, feel free to use the "SU" rows to keep notes.

The more organized you keep this column, the more organized your overall story and writing process will be. Of the many scenes you craft, not all of them will make it into the final cut of your final revision. Keeping track of your scenes and where they fall in the overall narrative becomes paramount, especially when you're searching later for a specific scene in a particular chapter. Rather than getting bogged down in the words as you skim for the chosen scene in your manuscript, you are able to scan your Scene Tracker for the exact location of the scene and continue working forward.

The notes you write in each box of the Scene Tracker need to be legible and memorable. Don't assume you'll remember your short-hand later. Be specific, and assign a meaning to every word and abbreviation so when you review the Scene Tracker for what's working and what's missing, your words immediately bring to mind how you used that particular element in that particular scene. The practice of creating a label that matches and stands for each element helps you pinpoint the main thrust, meaning, and development in the scene.

CASE STUDY: *ALL THE PRETTY HORSES*

National Book Award winner Cormac McCarthy's *All the Pretty Horses* begins in scene:

> The candleflame and the image of the candleflame caught in the pierglass twisted and righted when he entered the hall and again when he shut the door. He took off his hat and came slowly forward. The floorboards creaked under his boots. In his black suit he stood in the dark glass where the lilies leaned so palely from their waisted cutglass vase. Along the cold hallway behind him hung the portraits of forebears only dimly known to him all framed in glass and dimly lit above the narrow wainscotting. He looked down at the guttered candlestub. He pressed his thumbprint in the warm wax pooled on the oak veneer. Lastly he looked at the face so caved and drawn among the folds of funeral cloth, the yellowed moustache, the eyelids paper thin. That was not sleeping. That was not sleeping.
>
> It was dark outside and cold and no wind. In the distance a calf bawled. He stood with his hat in his hand. You never combed your hair that way in your life, he said.

Scene 1 from the first chapter continues for another page or so. We know it is a scene because the action is being played out moment by moment. The "candleflame" twists. He opens and closes the door and takes off his hat. The floorboards creak. These are all the makings of scene: immediacy, physicality, action.

In the Scene Tracker for this case study, I write "Ch. 1, SC 1" under Column One to indicate that this row will contain notes for the first scene in the first chapter. Noting the page number where the scene begins in your manuscript comes in handy later when you're looking for a specific scene.

Scene Tracker: *All the Pretty Horses* by Cormac McCarthy

SCENE (SC) OR SUMMARY (SU)	TIME AND SETTING	CHARACTER EMOTIONAL DEVELOPMENT	GOAL	DRAMATIC ACTION	CONFLICT	CHANGE	THEMATIC DETAILS
Ch. 1, SC 1							

◁▭▭▷ TRACK YOUR STORY

With your Scene Tracker in front of you, refer to your manuscript. Did you mark the beginning passage of your story as a scene or a summary? Whatever your answer, write the chapter number and "SC" or "SU" under the Scene or Summary Column. Do not worry about being right or wrong in your labeling at this point. As you work your way through your manuscript, you will be better able to determine scenes from summaries. For now, all that matters is that you have a passage to analyze.

If the first passage is a summary, mark "SU" under the Scene or Summary Column, and continue through your chapter until you find your first scene. Mark it on your Scene Tracker. This is the passage you will analyze.

If you tend to craft many short scenes rather than one longer one, consider tracking the actual chapter instead of each individual scene.

If you are writing a historical novel, the use of summary becomes critical, because this genre is generally longer and broader in scope than most contemporary fiction. Summary covers a relatively long period of time in a relatively short number of words.

A scene shows outward action. Scenes are in the now, the physical, chronicled moment by moment. Dialogue is a scene marker, as is action.

If you would rather continue with the task of filling in your Scene Tracker, move to chapter eighteen now. If you have questions about flashbacks, read on.

FLASHBACKS

At this point in a plot workshop, invariably a writer asks about flashbacks.

An agent once told me that, in her opinion, readers were no longer interested in stories told in chronological order. She believed that readers wish to be less passive and more interactive in the story, meaning that they were more interested in a nonlinear format. She might have come to this conclusion based on some of the popular fiction coming out at the time. For example, more than twenty years ago, Michael Ondaatje structured *The English Patient* in a nonlinear format; his story moves forward and backward in time and is chronicled by more than one character. A few years after the release of *The English Patient*, David Guterson formatted *Snow Falling on Cedars* by switching effortlessly from the front story to the backstory throughout the novel.

If you choose to write in a linear fashion, starting at the very beginning, you will seldom use flashbacks. However, if you want to try a nonlinear approach, or if you just do not want to start the story at the beginning, mastering flashbacks becomes critical.

Since the introduction of the nonlinear format, I have seen reader preferences revert back to chronological, linear storylines. For instance, Ursula Hegi begins *Stones from the River* with the protagonist's birth and tells everything that happens to the heroine, her village, and her country in sequence. Hegi uses no flashbacks because everything unfolds on the page as it happens in real story time.

Anita Diamant formats *The Red Tent* in essentially the same way, except the author starts with the mother's story and then, when her daughter is born, tells her story in chronological order. No scenes take place before the main action of the daughter's story.

Should you rely on flashbacks to tell your story, at least in part? To answer this question, you must first understand that story information is generally divided into two parts: the front story, which contains all the events that happen in scene as the story moves forward, and the backstory, which comprises all the history that makes the protagonist who she is today and why she sees the world in a particular way. The backstory helps the reader understand certain events and details in context. What happens *before* the events that take place on page 1 of the book is considered backstory. Every character has a backstory.

I believe that flashbacks, in which part of a character's backstory is revealed, are much abused. Sadly we too often confuse the information that is critical for the writer to know (such as the complete history of the character) with what is necessary to include in the text. When in doubt, writers too often revert to "telling" the backstory through the use of flashbacks.

A flashback is not the only way to include crucial backstory information. However, it is more difficult to *show* the backstory through the characters' actions and reactions, by their decision-making process and the consequences their choices reap. It is worth the effort to search for just the right details your character might notice or the few, well-chosen words she might use in the front story as a consequence of the backstory rather than resort to a flashback.

A flashback is a simple, though much abused, way to incorporate the backstory into the front story.

The careless use of flashbacks is one of the surest ways to break your reader from the trance. The last thing writers want to do is jar the reader from the dream they have so carefully crafted. This is what happens when you jump in time, either by taking a big leap forward or making a U-turn into the past in a flashback.

Keep in mind that when an event in the past is shown in moment-by-moment action, as if it is happening right now in the story, you're in a flashback. If the character is simply remembering an event in the past in summary, he's simply recalling a memory.

Using Flashbacks

"I write as straight as I can, just as I walk as straight as I can, because that is the best way to get there." –H.G. Wells

There are times when the effective use of a flashback will add significantly to the overall meaning of your story.

Flashbacks can be as short as one sentence, or they can be the longest part of the story. The one-liners can be incorporated through dialogue and description or as a memory without too much fear of impeding the forward movement of the story. Flashbacks that make up most of the story will essentially become, when well plotted, the forward-moving storyline. Incorporating intermediate flashbacks into the narrative can be far trickier.

A good rule of thumb is to only use flashbacks that appear above the line on your Plot Planner or those that contain important turning points in the character's development.

When you do use flashbacks, craft them in such a way that they are full of conflict, tension, and/or suspense. This is the best way to ensure that your flashbacks deliver only the essential information that informs the present action of the story and that pushes the story forward. A well-placed and well-crafted flashback can give the reader an important context to the main character's overall development.

Once you are convinced that a flashback is critical to the story, here are some ways to use flashbacks effectively:

1. Do not use too many of them—less is more.

2. Plot out your flashbacks, and give them their own conflict and tension. (Think of a flashback as a mini-story within the story.)
3. Bring in the past only when it has a direct bearing on what is happening in the present.
4. Start the story by firmly grounding the readers in the who, what, when, where, and why of the front story before going into a flashback.
5. Before you dive into the backstory, leave the reader with a memorable and authentic detail at a high or low place in the story. When you return to present time, use that detail again. This way, readers will recognize when they are leaving the front story for the backstory and when they are returning.
6. If you are writing your front story in present tense, then the flashback will be in simple past tense. (For example: "Times were not always this miserable. When we were small, we used to laugh until we cried.") If past tense is used for the primary action or the front story, then shift into past-perfect tense, using the word *had* for the flashback. (For example: "Times had not always been this miserable. When we had been small, we had laughed until we cried.") *Had* will alert the reader that the past is being introduced. If the flashback is long, use *had* once or twice to establish the time frame and continue with the simple past tense.
7. Use space breaks on either side of a flashback.
8. Explicitly mention the date or time when you enter the flashback, and mention the date and time of the present day when you leave the flashback.
9. If you feel that you *must* use a flashback, wait to use it in the middle of the story. By then, the reader has had time to become grounded in the front story and is more comfortable transitioning back and forth in time.
10. A flashback is portrayed moment by moment in scene. Consider if using a memory (summary) is more appropriate.
11. If flashbacks are integral to the overall plot and structure, do as Audrey Niffenegger does in *The Time Traveler's Wife*: Make the

storyline nonlinear and create the structure of your story based on time jumps.

If you have written a draft or two of your project and employed the use of flashbacks, take some time now to read over your work. The development of a flashback can be an opportunity for you as the writer to get to know your characters better. It's a chance to delve deeper into their essence or their history. Once you know that information, you can work to incorporate it in less intrusive ways into the story. See if you can come up with ways to weave important information into the front story without having to resort to the use of a flashback. If you no longer need the flashback, cut it.

If at any time during the tracking of your story you do come across a flashback, indicate that under the Scene/Summary Column. This way, you can track how many flashbacks you have and where they occur.

For example, if your story begins in flashback and the flashback is written in scene, then mark the Scene or Summary Column thus:

SCENE (SC) OR SUMMARY (SU)	TIME AND SETTING	CHARACTER EMOTIONAL DEVELOPMENT	GOAL	DRAMATIC ACTION	CONFLICT	CHANGE	THEMATIC DETAILS
Ch. 1, FLB, SC 1							

Chapter Eighteen

THE TIME AND SETTING COLUMN

The time and setting are two essential plot elements used in scene to help ground the reader in the here and now of the story.

By referencing the date—which can be the time of day, the week, the month, the year, or even the season—you help the reader settle into the now of the front story. Positioning your story in time allows the reader to detach from his real time, his immediate thoughts, and all the different directions he may be pulled in his real life to enter a different time—the time of the story.

Settings, in turn, fulfill a multitude of functions. One powerful purpose of the setting is to give the reader a sense of where she is and how life functions there when she is buried in the pages of the book. Settings are the center of the story. They invite the reader to let go of her own personal dramas and responsibilities, to calm her fears and worries, and to step into the place where the story action is occurring. Once the reader is firmly grounded in the setting, she is then able to move with confidence and certainty in whatever direction the story flows.

Be sure to ground your readers in the "where" and "when" of the scene. The last thing you want is for your reader to awaken from the dream you have so carefully crafted because he is disoriented or confused.

Relax. Creativity and inspiration never come from pushing.

CASE STUDY: *THE SEA-WOLF*

The following excerpt shows how one novelist integrates time and setting seamlessly into what's happening in the story.

The classic *The Sea-Wolf* by Jack London opens in circumstantial summary.

> I scarcely know where to begin, though I sometimes facetiously place the cause of it all to Charley Furuseth's credit. He kept a summer cottage in Mill Valley, under the shadow of Mount Tamalpais, and never occupied it except when he loafed through the winter months and read Nietzsche and Schopenhauer to rest his brain. When summer came on, he elected to sweat out a hot and dusty existence in the city and to toil incessantly. Had it not been my custom to run up to see him every Saturday afternoon and to stop over till Monday morning, this particular January Monday morning would not have found me afloat on San Francisco Bay.

Many works of literary fiction begin with a description in summary of the story's ordinary world to give the reader a feel of the time. We know *The Sea-Wolf* begins in summary, because in the passage the character is not taking us through the action moment by moment. He is telling us, or describing, the general circumstances during this period: how things were, the sorts of things that usually or frequently happened, and what put him in his current situation.

Therefore, on the Scene Tracker we mark in Column 1 "SU" for Summary. Feel free to note in the Time and Setting column that the summary tells that it is January on a Monday morning. Don't add anymore than that, because we do not track summary information on the Scene Tracker. We only track the scenes.

Scene Tracker: *The Sea-Wolf* by Jack London

SCENE (SC) OR SUMMARY (SU)	TIME AND SETTING	CHARACTER EMOTIONAL DEVELOPMENT	GOAL	DRAMATIC ACTION	CONFLICT	CHANGE IN EMOTION	THEMATIC DETAILS
Ch. 1, SU							

London begins the fourth paragraph of chapter one as follows.

> A red-faced man, slamming the cabin door behind him and stumping out
> on the deck, interrupted my reflections, though I made a mental note of
> the topic for use in a projected essay which I had thought of calling "The
> Necessity for Freedom: A Plea for the Artist." The red-faced man shot a
> glance up at the pilot-house, gazed around at the fog, stumped across the
> deck and back (he evidently had artificial legs), and stood still by my side,
> legs wide apart, and with an expression of keen enjoyment on his face. I
> was not wrong when I decided that his days had been spent on the sea.

Now we can begin tracking because we have come to the beginning
of an actual scene. The first scene of chapter one continues for almost seven pages. We know it is a scene because the action is being
played out moment by moment. For this case study, because the date
indicated in the summary passage still applies, we add it to the "Ch.
1, SC 1" row.

Scene Tracker: *The Sea-Wolf* by Jack London

SCENE (SC) OR SUMMARY (SU)	TIME AND SETTING	CHARACTER EMOTIONAL DEVELOPMENT	GOAL	DRAMATIC ACTION	CONFLICT	CHANGE IN EMOTION	THEMATIC DETAILS
Ch. 1, SU							
Ch. 1, SC 1	Jan. Mon. A.M.						

CASE STUDY: *ALL THE PRETTY HORSES*

In the paragraph following the opening passage, McCarthy writes in
All the Pretty Horses: "… a thin gray reef beginning along the eastern
rim of the world …" Thus all we know about the timing is that the
scene takes place just before dawn.

Scene Tracker: *All the Pretty Horses* by Cormac McCarthy

SCENE (SC) OR SUMMARY (SU)	TIME AND SETTING	CHARACTER EMOTIONAL DEVELOPMENT	GOAL	DRAMATIC ACTION	CONFLICT	CHANGE IN EMOTION	THEMATIC DETAILS

Ch. 1, SC 1	Just before dawn						

⊂▭▷ TRACKING YOUR STORY

With your Scene Tracker in front of you, refer back to your manuscript. Fill in the Time and Setting Column with when your story begins—the season, year, and/or time of day. Include any real-life historical events and political issues that occur during this time and have an affect on your plot.

Even if your story does not directly involve true historical events, one way to add more depth to your story is to include at least one major and one minor historical event, as well as a trivial event. This will provide you with a perspective of what is happening in the setting, country, and world during the time period in which you are writing. Historical events, especially the major ones, can provide useful information with which to thicken the plot.

For example, the historical novel I am currently writing begins in February 1968, a time of cataclysmic upheaval in the United States, a time in history when the great divide of class and culture no longer kept people separated, however different they might be. For the purpose of my Scene Tracker, I abbreviate this historical period as "Great Divide" and add it under the date. Following that is a more specific historical event: the first United Farm Workers Benefit held at Fillmore West in San Francisco, which I abbreviate as "UFW."

Scene Tracker: *Parallel Lives* by Martha Alderson

SCENE (SC) OR SUMMARY (SU)	TIME AND SETTING	CHARACTER EMOTIONAL DEVELOPMENT	GOAL	DRAMATIC ACTION	CONFLICT	CHANGE IN EMOTION	THEMATIC DETAILS
Ch. 1, SC 1	Feb. 1968 Great Divide UFW						

Instead of waiting for inspiration to hit, show up to write and plot at the same time every day. Inspiration will follow.

If you would like to continue tracking your scenes, move now to chapter nineteen. If you wish to read more about the benefits of research, continue to the end of this chapter.

RESEARCHING TIME PERIODS AND SETTINGS

Research is critical for historical fiction writers, but I contend that it is crucial for all other genres as well. You (and your readers) benefit from thoroughly researching the time period and setting in which you are writing. Even if you are writing about a time in which you lived, be it in memoir or fiction form, you cannot rely on memory alone.

Stories that tell the truth are firmly grounded in research.

If you find yourself lapsing into the use of clichés or, worse, perpetuating the generalizations, prejudices, and oversimplifications we complacently assume every day, delve deeper into the world of your story through research to reveal the truth. If you find yourself stopped by writer's block, plumb the world of your story through research and the block will often dissolve.

Research must be woven in artfully.

If your research involves too many details, then indicate where to find the files in which the relevant facts and details are located. Be as clear and specific as you can about the information, both on the notes and in the actual files. The creation of a novel can take months and years, and there is nothing as frustrating as coming across an incomplete scribble that makes no sense when you need to access an important detail or fact.

Whenever possible, write your research on sticky notes and organize your findings on your Scene Tracker.

A word of caution: The use of research is as dicey as the use of flashback. Every bit of fascinating information you uncover does not belong in the book unless it contributes to the overall plot, be it the action plotline, the character plotline, or the thematic plotline.

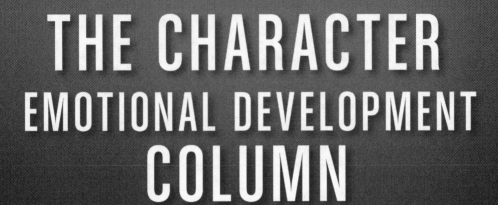

Chapter Nineteen

THE CHARACTER EMOTIONAL DEVELOPMENT COLUMN

The information you include in the Scene Tracker boxes in the Character Emotional Development Column tracks the Character Emotional Development plot scene by scene. Thus what you write in these boxes for the beginning scenes will be vastly different emotional information about the character compared to what you convey about his emotional makeup in the middle scenes and the end scenes.

For the beginning scenes, make a note of which scenes you *introduce* various character emotional and personality traits. Refer to the protagonist's Character Emotional Development Profile to determine the primary traits to introduce in creating a multidimensional and emotional character. Since you're attempting to engage the reader with the character, you'll likely demonstrate mostly positive traits. However, to make the character believable, he must have traits he struggles with. If your story involves a character that experiences an internal transformation by the end, take the opportunity as early as you can in the beginning to at least hint at his "fatal" flaw—the personality trait that will ultimately play a part in his downfall at the crisis.

In the scenes in the middle, you'll *deepen* the reader's appreciation of the traits introduced in the beginning as the character is put under more and more strain, stress, and pressure.

In the end scenes, show how the character acts and reacts now that he has *transformed* emotionally in comparison to how he acted and reacted in the beginning and in the middle. Show how his emotional development serves him now at the end.

We begin this chapter with examples of how to track beginning scenes.

CASE STUDY: *WHITE OLEANDER*

Janet Fitch begins *White Oleander* in scene.

> The Santa Anas blew in hot from the desert, shriveling the last of the spring grass into whiskers of pale straw. Only the oleanders thrived, their delicate poisonous blooms, their dagger green leaves. We could not sleep in the hot dry nights, my mother and I. I woke up at midnight to find her bed empty. I climbed to the roof and easily spotted her blond hair like a white flame in the light of the three-quarter moon.
>
> "Oleander time," she said. "Lovers who kill each other now will blame it on the wind." She held up her large hand and spread the fingers, let the desert dryness lick through. My mother was not herself in the time of the Santa Anas. I was twelve years old and I was afraid for her. I wished things were back the way they had been, that Barry was still here. That the wind would stop blowing.
>
> "You should get some sleep," I offered.
>
> "I never sleep," she said.

Scene Tracker: *White Oleander* by Janet Fitch

SCENE (SC) OR SUMMARY (SU)	TIME AND SETTING	CHARACTER EMOTIONAL DEVELOPMENT	GOAL	DRAMATIC ACTION	CONFLICT	CHANGE IN EMOTION	THEMATIC DETAILS
Ch. 1, SC 1	Nighttime Santa Ana	Deeply identifies with mother; 12 years old; afraid; takes care of mother					

The first scene of chapter one of *White Oleander* is a page and a half. We know it is a scene because the action is played out moment by moment. Though the narrator says very little about herself directly, we learn several important details about her character emotional development in this passage:

> We could not sleep in the hot dry nights, my mother and I.

This sentence speaks volumes: It shows how deeply the narrator identifies with her mother.

> I climbed to the roof …

Again, in showing this action, we understand how connected these two characters are. The child knows from experience just where to find her mother on a night like tonight.

> I was twelve years old and I was afraid for her.

> "You should get some sleep," I offered.

CASE STUDY: *ALL THE PRETTY HORSES*

In scene one, there is little to inform us about the protagonist other than his statement at the end of the second paragraph.

> You never combed your hair that way in your life, he said.

From these simple words, we get the sense that he is observant and speaks the truth.

Scene Tracker: *All the Pretty Horses* by Cormac McCarthy

SCENE (SC) OR SUMMARY (SU)	TIME AND SETTING	CHARACTER EMOTIONAL DEVELOPMENT	GOAL	DRAMATIC ACTION	CONFLICT	CHANGE IN EMOTION	THEMATIC DETAILS
Ch. 1, SC 1	Just before dawn	Speaks the truth					

"Unless I know what sort of doorknob his fingers closed on, how shall I—satisfactorily to myself—get my character out of doors?" –Ford Madox Ford

CASE STUDY: *THE SEA-WOLF*

In the first scene, we find out that the protagonist has a tendency to blame others for his misfortunes. In the opening summary and scene one, we learn that he is intelligent, that he likes to hang out weekly with a man who loafs about by reading Nietzsche and Schopenhauer, and that he is a writer.

Scene Tracker: *The Sea-Wolf* by Jack London							
SCENE (SC) OR SUMMARY (SU)	TIME AND SETTING	CHARACTER EMOTIONAL DEVELOPMENT	GOAL	DRAMATIC ACTION	CONFLICT	CHANGE IN EMOTION	THEMATIC DETAILS
Ch. 1, SU							
Ch. 1, SC 1	Jan. Mon. A.M.	Blames others; intelligent; writer					

⟞▷ TRACKING YOUR STORY

With your Scene Tracker in front of you, refer to your manuscript and fill in the Character Emotional Development Column with any significant character traits brought forward in your scenes. This is also the place where you indicate any important character background information you want to keep in mind about the protagonist.

If you have two major point-of-view characters (two protagonists), or if you want to track the antagonist as well as the protagonist, just use different-colored pens for each of them.

When filling out the Character Emotional Development column, watch for the flaws of your protagonist to come to light. For example, is your protagonist a procrastinator or a perfectionist? Is she judgmental, greedy, bullheaded, pessimistic, or jealous?

At the same time, search for your protagonist's strengths. As much as his flaw creates tension, his strengths and spunk are attributes that make readers want to stick with him through his problems.

The Role of Adversity

As stated earlier, the middle (one-half of the entire project) serves to reveal the deeper nuances of the character's emotional development. This is the part of the story where the writer thrusts the protagonist into as much adversity as possible in order to reveal to the reader who the character really is.

Make a list of all possible antagonists–other people, nature, society, a belief system, machines, etc.–that can help generate conflict, tension, suspense, or curiosity and thus reveal who the character is under pressure. The more pressure the better.

The end (the last quarter of the project) actually shows how the character's emotional development has been affected by the adversity in the middle and reveals how the character has been changed or transformed. Though your character will demonstrate the new behavior and act with his newfound understanding, based on what happened in the crisis, he will not do so consistently at first. Full mastery at the deepest level comes only at the climax.

These steps in the overall character emotional transformation can be plotted on a Scene Tracker for ease in developing your project.

A successful writer writes every day, even if for only ten minutes.

Chapter Twenty

THE GOAL COLUMN

The character's long-term goal drives the external dramatic action of the story. Her pursuit of her long-term goal ultimately leads her to change, grow, mature, and transform. The character also needs a goal in every scene. She may or may not even approach that goal by scene's end, but the reader needs to know what the character is up to at all times. Hence the Goal Column in the Scene Tracker is used to note, in an abbreviated form, the protagonist's goal at the start of every scene. These scene goals are not *your* goals for the character, but the *protagonist's*. They are the specific steps she plans to take that she believes will help advance her toward her ultimate goal.

What does the protagonist want? This question poses a challenge to many writers, but unless the protagonist wants something specific in every scene, the scene and story wander.

For scenes in the beginning of the story, you'll indicate in the Goal Column the steps she takes toward her ultimate goal. Usually by the end of the first quarter of the story, the protagonist has been forced, coerced, or convinced to let go of her attachment to the familiar, the safe, and the comfortable. When she arrives in the middle, you'll summarize her long-term goal and indicate on the Scene Tracker how this change causes her short-term scene goals to change.

After the crisis, her goals generally change again. As the character's goals become riskier, more difficult to attain, more dangerous to pursue, or trickier to achieve, the reader has to believe that the character will continue even in the face of peril. Use the Goal Column to indicate what you conveyed in each scene related to the character's motivation. These are the reasons why she has the goals she has and takes the actions she takes.

Here are some common driving motivations:

- increase or loss of material well-being
- an authority
- making amends
- love
- criminal action (including murder)
- solving a mystery
- searching for something significant, valuable, meaningful, or necessary
- honor and dishonor
- fulfilling a destiny
- desire
- safety
- revenge

Track her motivation in addition to her scene goals, and, when appropriate, include where, when, why, and how her motivation shifts and changes.

The difference between a dream and a goal is that a goal is quantifiable. To achieve your writing goals, make them small and achievable.

CASE STUDY: *WHERE THE HEART IS*

The following scene demonstrates how a character's goals are expressed without the character stating what she wants explicitly. Those goals are then inserted into the Goal Column on the Scene Tracker grid.

In the opening scene of Billie Letts's *Where the Heart Is*, we learn about the protagonist.

> Novalee Nation, seventeen, seven months pregnant, thirty-seven pounds overweight—and superstitious about sevens—shifted uncomfortably in the seat of the old Plymouth and ran her hands down the curve of her belly.

Three paragraphs later the protagonist's scene goal is made abundantly clear.

> But she didn't have sevens on her mind as she twisted and squirmed, trying to compromise with a hateful pain pressing against her pelvis. She needed to stop again, but it was too soon to ask. They had stopped once since Fort Smith, but already Novalee's bladder felt like a water balloon.

Scene Tracker: *Where the Heart Is* by Billie Letts							
SCENE (SC) OR SUMMARY (SU)	TIME AND SETTING	CHARACTER EMOTIONAL DEVELOPMENT	GOAL	DRAMATIC ACTION	CONFLICT	CHANGE IN EMOTION	THEMATIC DETAILS
Ch. 1, SC 1	In a car headed for CA	17 yrs. old; 7 months preg- nant; supersti- tious about sevens	To use the restroom				

Sometimes a scene's beginning and end are not clear-cut and thus become subjective. The first scene of *Where the Heart Is* might be considered the entire first chapter, a total of fourteen pages. We know it is a scene because the action is being played out moment by moment. But a dream sequence lies in the middle of chapter one, so you might decide that the dream marks the end of scene one and the beginning of scene two. Or the moment Novalee walks into Walmart could be the marker. How you decide where a scene begins and ends in your project is not always an exact science. For our purposes here, it matters less how you decide on these parameters and more how you justify your decision to yourself for tracking purposes.

Throughout the first fourteen pages of *Where the Heart Is*, we are with Novalee moment by moment. At times, Letts interrupts the *showing* to *tell* us information about Novalee's past, but the telling is always within the context of the action going on in the scene. For our purposes, I have made the decision that scene one ends when she enters Walmart.

Either way, Letts establishes Novalee's goal at the very beginning of the scene, and tension is created immediately because the reader knows that something needs to happen soon or Novalee will be in trouble. In the same way that we are shown Novalee's goal and her motivation to relieve her discomfort, we are also shown that her boyfriend has the completely opposing goal to keep driving.

Beware of the trap of discussing your story too much with others. Instead use all your energy for the actual writing. It is possible to kill a story–the punch of it, your passion for it–by talking it to death.

CASE STUDY: *ALL THE PRETTY HORSES*

In the opening scene, there is little to inform us about the character's scene goal and why he is where he is. Therefore, we leave this box blank.

Scene Tracker: *All the Pretty Horses* by Cormac McCarthy

SCENE (SC) OR SUMMARY (SU)	TIME AND SETTING	CHARACTER EMOTIONAL DEVELOPMENT	GOAL	DRAMATIC ACTION	CONFLICT	CHANGE IN EMOTION	THEMATIC DETAILS
Ch. 1, SC 1	Just before dawn	Speaks the truth					

CASE STUDY: *THE SEA-WOLF*

We learn in scene one that the protagonist intends to write an essay titled "The Necessity for Freedom: A Plea for the Artist."

Scene Tracker: *The Sea-Wolf* by Jack London

SCENE (SC) OR SUMMARY (SU)	TIME AND SETTING	CHARACTER EMOTIONAL DEVELOPMENT	GOAL	DRAMATIC ACTION	CONFLICT	CHANGE IN EMOTION	THEMATIC DETAILS
Ch. 1, SU							

Ch. 1, SC 1	Jan. Mon. A.M.	Blames oth- ers; intelligent; writer	Write essay					

CASE STUDY: *WHITE OLEANDER*

We learn of the protagonist's goals from her narrative in scene one:

> **LONG-TERM STORY GOAL:** "I wished things were back the way they had been."
>
> **SHORT-TERM SCENE GOAL:** "You should get some sleep," I offered.

For our purposes, we mark only the short-term scene goal on the Scene Tracker.

Scene Tracker: *White Oleander* by Janet Fitch

SCENE (SC) OR SUMMARY (SU)	TIME AND SETTING	CHARACTER EMOTIONAL DEVELOPMENT	GOAL	DRAMATIC ACTION	CONFLICT	CHANGE IN EMOTION	THEMATIC DETAILS
Ch. 1, SC 1	Nighttime Santa Ana	Deeply identifies with mother; 12 years old; afraid; takes care of mother	Give mother comfort				

✏️ TRACKING YOUR STORY

With your Scene Tracker in front of you, refer to your manuscript and fill in the Goal Column with the protagonist's goal in the scene.

The short-term scene goals and long-term story goals do not have to be plainly stated, but they do have to be at least implied. A short-term goal gives direction to the scene. Without it, a scene loses its significance and tends to ramble. The protagonist must always be working toward something. Conflict is created by all the factors that prevent her from achieving her short-term scene goals and, ultimately, her long-term goal.

Creating both short-term and long-term goals for the protagonist is difficult for many writers. Stick with it. Readers stay with a story to see if the protagonist is going to achieve or accomplish what she wants in life. Suspense is the state of anticipation, wanting to know what happens next.

By having the protagonist want something of utmost importance, the reader knows what is at stake.

Often the protagonist's desire rules her entire life only to find in the end that her desire does not bring satisfaction.

Chapter Twenty-One

THE DRAMATIC ACTION COLUMN

Moment-by-moment dramatic action makes up the next layer of scene. Dramatic action is one of the three primary plotlines and is a major essential element in developing scenes.

Embedded within this layer ideally lies a layer (or two or three or four) of conflict, tension, suspense, and curiosity. I say "ideally" because though the column is labeled "dramatic action" to emphasize the importance of keeping the action exciting, not all action in every scene is dramatic.

The Dramatic Action Column does not ask you to determine whether the action in the scene is dramatic. Simply note what action happens in the scene, whether passive or dramatic, or above the line or below the line. If the scene consists purely of dialogue, write "talking" in bold letters to make that notation stand out from the others. That way you can quickly spot and assess how much talking your characters do without taking action and, when you begin your rewrite, you can be sure to incorporate dramatic action in those scenes.

Action needs conflict in order to be dramatic. Begin by tracking the conflict in every scene. In the Dramatic Action Column on the Scene Tracker, you will declare whether the action is inherently dramatic due to conflict. This column relates directly to the Change in Emotion Column (see chapter twenty-three), which tracks the immediate effect that action has on the character as seen through her emotional change, response, or reaction.

CASE STUDY: *THE ADVENTURES OF TOM SAWYER*

The following scene begins Mark Twain's *The Adventures of Tom Sawyer*.

"Tom!"

No answer. "Tom!"

No answer.

"What's gone with that boy, I wonder? You Tom!" No answer.

The old lady pulled her spectacles down and looked over them about the room; then she put them up and looked out under them. She seldom or never looked through them for so small a thing as a boy; they were her state pair, the pride of her heart, and were built for "style," not service—she could have seen through a pair of stove-lids just as well. She looked perplexed for a moment, and then said, not fiercely, but still loud enough for the furniture to hear:

"Well, I lay if I get hold of you I'll—"

She did not finish, for by this time she was bending down and punching under the bed with the broom, and so she needed breath to punctuate the punches with. She resurrected nothing but the cat.

"I never did see the beat of that boy!"

She went to the open door and stood in it and looked out among the tomato vines and "jimpson" weeds that constituted the garden. No Tom. So she lifted up her voice at an angle calculated for distance and shouted:

"Y-o-u-u Tom!"

There was a slight noise behind her and she turned just in time to seize a small boy by the slack of his roundabout and arrest his flight.

"There! I might 'a' thought of that closet. What you been doing in there?"

"Nothing."

"Nothing! Look at your hands. And look at your mouth. What is that truck?"

"I don't know, aunt."

"Well, I know. It's jam—that's what it is. Forty times I've said if you didn't let that jam alone I'd skin you. Hand me that switch."

The switch hovered in the air—the peril was desperate—

"My! Look behind you, aunt!"

The old lady whirled round, and snatched her skirts out of danger.

The lad fled on the instant, scrambled up the high board-fence, and disappeared over it.

Scene Tracker: *The Adventures of Tom Sawyer* by Mark Twain								
SCENE (SC) OR SUMMARY (SU)	TIME AND SETTING	CHARACTER EMOTIONAL DEVELOPMENT	GOAL	DRAMATIC ACTION	CONFLICT	CHANGE IN EMOTION	THEMATIC DETAILS
Ch. 1, SC 1	Fri. Aunt's house	T: Small, smart, fast, liar A: took in dead sister's son	Escape	Tom/Aunt trouble			

By now you are likely able to identify this passage as a scene. The passage is made up of definite action and dialogue, and unfolds in such a way that the reader is able to slip into the scene and actually experience the excitement moment to moment.

The passage doesn't indicate the year, season, or time of day, but we do know it is Friday and that the scene takes place at the aunt's house.

The first character introduced is the aunt, but since we know that Tom is the protagonist, we write his information under Character Emotional Development first and the aunt's information below it in a different color.

From the aunt's monologue, we learn that Tom is a small boy, fast both in mind and on his feet, and that he is a liar. His goal in this scene is to escape. For the purposes of the Scene Tracker, I abbreviate the action to "Tom/Aunt trouble."

Look for ways to heighten conflict, tension, suspense, and/or curiosity in every scene you write.

CASE STUDY: *ALL THE PRETTY HORSES*

All the Pretty Horses opens in scene, so action must be present in some form. The action in the first paragraph shows the character entering a house where a dead man is laid out for viewing.

Scene Tracker: *All the Pretty Horses* by Cormac McCarthy

SCENE (SC) OR SUMMARY (SU)	TIME AND SETTING	CHARACTER EMOTIONAL DEVELOPMENT	GOAL	DRAMATIC ACTION	CONFLICT	CHANGE IN EMOTION	THEMATIC DETAILS
Ch. 1, SC 1	Just before dawn	Speaks the truth		View of dead man			

CASE STUDY: *THE SEA-WOLF*

In *The Sea-Wolf*, the dramatic action thus far is limited to the appearance of the red-faced stranger.

Scene Tracker: *The Sea-Wolf* by Jack London

SCENE (SC) OR SUMMARY (SU)	TIME AND SETTING	CHARACTER EMOTIONAL DEVELOPMENT	GOAL	DRAMATIC ACTION	CONFLICT	CHANGE IN EMOTION	THEMATIC DETAILS
Ch. 1, SU							
Ch. 1, SC 1	Jan. Mon. A.M.	Blames others; intelligent; writer	Write essay	Stranger appears			

CASE STUDY: *WHITE OLEANDER*

The action of the opening scene primarily revolves around the daughter climbing to the roof to find her mother.

Scene Tracker: *White Oleander* by Janet Fitch

SCENE (SC) OR SUMMARY (SU)	TIME AND SETTING	CHARACTER EMOTIONAL DEVELOPMENT	GOAL	DRAMATIC ACTION	CONFLICT	CHANGE IN EMOTION	THEMATIC DETAILS
Ch. 1, SC 1	Nighttime Santa Ana	Deeply identifies with mother; 12 years old; afraid; takes care of mother	Give mother comfort	Roof w/ mother			

CASE STUDY: *WHERE THE HEART IS*

The action of the first scene is limited to sitting, albeit uncomfortably, in the front seat of a car headed for California.

Scene Tracker: *Where the Heart Is* by Billie Letts

SCENE (SC) OR SUMMARY (SU)	DATE AND SETTING	CHARACTER EMOTIONAL DEVELOPMENT	GOAL	DRAMATIC ACTION	CONFLICT	CHANGE IN EMOTION	THEMATIC DETAILS
Ch. 1, SC 1	In a car headed for CA	17 yrs. old; 7 months pregnant; superstitious about sevens	To use the restroom	Riding in a car			

◁▭▭▷ TRACKING YOUR STORY

With your Scene Tracker in front of you, refer to your manuscript. Indicate under the Dramatic Action Column what action takes place in your scenes. Sum up the action in the scene as succinctly as possible.

Since a scene is not truly a scene unless it has some sort of conflict, tension, or suspense–real or imagined–try to include the pivotal conflict in the Dramatic Action Column description.

As I explained in the Flashback section of chapter seventeen, story information is generally divided into two parts: the front story and the backstory. The front story contains all the action that happens in scene as the story moves forward. The backstory is made up of all the history that makes the characters who they are today and causes them to see the world as they do. The backstory helps the reader to understand things in context. (Backstory was discussed in more depth in chapter seventeen.)

If your story begins with a summary, it may not contain any dramatic action and therefore you won't be able to write anything on your Scene Tracker. Summary is telling, and so it does not usually involve dramatic action. However, *every* scene involves action that moves the front story forward. The action-driven plotline is the front story—the physical events unfolding in a dramatic and exciting way on the page. As you track your story, ensure that the action focuses on the front story and can be considered dramatic.

Chapter Twenty-Two

THE CONFLICT COLUMN

Conflict and risks that involve tense and suspenseful action shake a story. Without conflict, a story doesn't move. When a story doesn't move, the character doesn't grow. The significance of conflict earns it an important place in the essential elements of scene.

We discussed the Dramatic Action Column in the last chapter. The Conflict Column discussed in this chapter serves as yet another test to determine whether the action in each scene is dramatic or passive. We covered the need for conflict and how to go about creating tense situations in an overall plot in the Plot Planner section of this book. Now we want to examine the dramatic action in each of the scenes we filled in under the Dramatic Action Column, searching for conflict, beginning with the case studies. Then you'll be asked to track the conflict in your scenes.

CASE STUDY: *THE ADVENTURES OF TOM SAWYER*

Our example from the previous chapter, the first scene in Mark Twain's *The Adventures of Tom Sawyer*, contains conflict. The reader does not yet know that Tom's aunt is a softy and would never actually use the switch on Tom. So, as her frustration grows because she is unable to find him, the reader anticipates that this mischievous boy is going to get a whipping for not answering her and for hiding out and eating the jam. There is no reason for the reader not to believe her when she threatens: "Well, I lay if I get hold of you I'll—" By using phrases such as "seize a small boy by the slack of his roundabout and arrest his flight," Twain sets us up to believe that this "small boy" is in for it.

Note the active verbs–*seize* and *arrest*. These verbs work on the surface of providing action and also on an implied level of what must be coming.

As the story continues, it becomes obvious that the boy is lying:

> "There! I might 'a' thought of that closet. What you been doing in there?"
> "Nothing."
> "Nothing! Look at your hands. And look at your mouth. What is that truck?"
> "I don't know, aunt."

Of course he knows. And the reader knows he knows, and fears for him, because lying can cause dire consequences. Twain goes on to put an actual threat in the mouth of the aunt, and we know disaster is imminent.

> Well, I know. It's jam—that's what it is. Forty times I've said if you didn't let that jam alone I'd skin you. Hand me that switch."
> The switch hovered in the air—the peril was desperate—

Scene Tracker: *The Adventures of Tom Sawyer* by Mark Twain

SCENE (SC) OR SUMMARY (SU)	TIME AND SETTING	CHARACTER EMOTIONAL DEVELOPMENT	GOAL	DRAMATIC ACTION	CONFLICT	CHANGE IN EMOTION	THEMATIC DETAILS
Ch. 1, SC 1	Fri. Aunt's house	T: Small, smart, fast, liar A: took in dead sister's son	Escape	Tom/Aunt trouble	X		

This scene is crafted to keep the reader in suspense by creating conflict on several levels at once. Therefore, an X goes under the Conflict Column, indicating that there is indeed conflict and tension in this scene.

CASE STUDY: *ALL THE PRETTY HORSES*

Since *All the Pretty Horses* opens in scene, not only must there be action of some sort, there must also be some sort of conflict, tension, or suspense. This tension is implied by what comes at the end of the action itself. A dead man laid out for viewing creates curiosity and a certain suspense that forces the reader to read on to discover who died, what caused his death, and what that means to the overall story.

Scene Tracker: *All the Pretty Horses* by Cormac McCarthy

SCENE (SC) OR SUMMARY (SU)	TIME AND SETTING	CHARACTER EMOTIONAL DEVELOPMENT	GOAL	DRAMATIC ACTION	CONFLICT	CHANGE IN EMOTION	THEMATIC DETAILS
Ch. 1, SC 1	Just before dawn	Speaks the truth		View of dead man	X		

CASE STUDY: *THE SEA-WOLF*

Jack London gives us a hint of what is to come when he closes the first paragraph: "… found me afloat on the San Francisco Bay," a phrase that creates curiosity and suspense that forces the reader to read on. Also, whenever a stranger appears, tension is created because the reader wants to know who the stranger is and the part he will play in the story.

Scene Tracker: *The Sea-Wolf* by Jack London

SCENE (SC) OR SUMMARY (SU)	TIME AND SETTING	CHARACTER EMOTIONAL DEVELOPMENT	GOAL	DRAMATIC ACTION	CONFLICT	CHANGE IN EMOTION	THEMATIC DETAILS
Ch. 1, SU							
Ch. 1, SC 1	Jan. Mon. A.M.	Blames others; intelligent; writer	Write essay	Stranger appears	X		

The best way to improve your writing is by reading.

CASE STUDY: *WHITE OLEANDER*

Not much tension is produced by the action itself, since the action of the scene primarily revolves around the daughter climbing to the roof to find her mother. However, throughout the scene the author sets the tone of the story and hits the reader repeatedly with hints and details that foreshadow what is to come. For instance:

> Only the oleanders thrived, their delicate poisonous blooms, their dagger green leaves.

> "Lovers who kill each other now will blame it on the wind."

> I was afraid for her.
> … that the wind would stop blowing.

The scene continues for another page, and the foreshadowing continues, full of ominous "telling" details, all of which create a sense of doom of what is to come.

Scene Tracker: *White Oleander* by Janet Fitch

SCENE (SC) OR SUMMARY (SU)	TIME AND SETTING	CHARACTER EMOTIONAL DEVELOPMENT	GOAL	DRAMATIC ACTION	CONFLICT	CHANGE IN EMOTION	THEMATIC DETAILS
Ch. 1, SC 1	Nighttime Santa Ana	Deeply identifies with mother; 12 years old; afraid; takes care of mother	Give mother comfort	Roof w/ mother	X		

CASE STUDY: *WHERE THE HEART IS*

Though the action of the scene in *Where the Heart Is* is limited to sitting, albeit uncomfortably, in the front seat of a car headed for California, the author creates tension in the fact that Novalee is not speaking up for herself and thus is not achieving her goal. The reader reads on, curious as to what is standing in Novalee's way. It does not take long for the reader to learn that Novalee fears the antagonist in this scene, her boyfriend.

Scene Tracker: *Where the Heart Is* by Billie Letts

SCENE (SC) OR SUMMARY (SU)	TIME AND SETTING	CHARACTER EMOTIONAL DEVELOPMENT	GOAL	DRAMATIC ACTION	CONFLICT	CHANGE IN EMOTION	THEMATIC DETAILS
Ch. 1, SC 1	In a car headed for CA	17 yrs. old; 7 months pregnant; superstitious about sevens	To use the restroom	Riding in a car	X		

⫐▭▭▷ TRACKING YOUR STORY

With your Scene Tracker in front of you, refer to your manuscript and mark an X in the Conflict Column if conflict, tension, or suspense is present in the first scene of your project. As you scan your Scene Tracker, you'll be able to quickly assess how many scenes have dramatic action and, more important, how many scenes do not. Seeing the big picture of your story noted on your Scene Tracker gives you an immediate sense of where to focus your attention in your next rewrite. Some writers choose to write a brief summary of the conflict or a list of details about the conflict in the box. Other writers assign the conflict a number between 1 and 10, with 10 carrying the most conflict and drama. Remember that there is no right or wrong way to use the Scene Tracker. At any time, feel free to adapt this tool to suit your individual needs.

Janet Burroway writes in *Writing Fiction: A Guide to Narrative Craft* that "conflict … is the fundamental element of fiction, necessary because in literature, only trouble is interesting."

Story is conflict shown in scene, and conflict is what makes readers turn the page. Yet one of the most common problems writers struggle with in my plot workshops and private consultations is that the conflict in their stories is flat, there's not enough conflict, or the conflict is inconsistent. Without some sort of conflict, you do not have a scene or, for that matter, a story.

Conflict does not have to be overt, but it must be there in some form of suspense or the result of something unknown lurking in the shadows. These elements are built through setbacks, not through good news.

I covered conflict in more detail in Part One of this book. For our purposes, I want you to determine if there is conflict in the scene or summary you are analyzing. Summary does not always have conflict, which is another reason not to overuse summary in your stories. Scenes at their best always contain some sort of conflict.

Tips for Creating Conflict

When deciding on your story problem, use the tension of the action that is unfolding center stage as a reflection of the protagonist's internal tension. Be sure to show this internal tension through action and reaction in scene, thereby avoiding too much telling through internal monologue.

For each scene, ask yourself the following questions:

- Where is the conflict?
- Who is the conflict between?
- What is causing the conflict?
- How much tension is caused by the conflict?
- How can more tension be created?

The following list shows a few of the many ways you can heighten the conflict in your story through the use of your character's psychology:

1. Show something or someone your protagonist loves being threatened. This will force your protagonist to make a decision and act on it. Raise the stakes and increase the threat in the next scene in order to create "rising conflict."
2. In real life, most of us avoid conflict at all costs. But this shouldn't be your philosophy when telling stories. People read stories to see how characters grow and change, even if this change and growth is not for the better. Turn up the pressure on your story characters. Put your protagonist in the middle of what he hates the most and then show the choices he makes in his attempt to avoid, change, or escape it.

3. Show, in scene, your protagonist taking center stage alongside his greatest fear.
4. Establish your protagonist's dream and then show him constantly sabotaging that dream by the choices made based on his character flaw.

The choices the protagonist makes create the action. Both the character and the action will ultimately reflect the underlying theme of your story, the thematic plot. With this interweaving of character, action, and theme, the story you create will be rich in character and conflict, making for a compelling and satisfying page-turner.

By using something within the character's psychology to create tension or conflict, you create a multilayered plotline, one involving character growth (the emotional plot) directly linked to the action (the dramatic plot).

Chapter Twenty-Three

THE CHANGE
IN
EMOTION COLUMN

Just as the conflict in every scene affects the overall emotional growth of your characters throughout the entire work, the dramatic action in each scene affects and changes your characters' emotional states on a moment-by-moment basis. I'm not necessarily referring to lasting emotions but to mood changes that fluctuate, and rise and fall, in correspondence with what was said or done in a specific scene. These emotions are experienced in the moment and are not permanent. They are a result of feelings that come and go based on the character's circumstances and her internal state and are often experienced through the senses.

To make your characters real and relatable, and the action true and impactful, show how the character's emotional state changes from the beginning of the scene, through the middle of the scene, and at the end of the scene. All of us go through a multitude of emotions throughout a day. It is not normal for someone to feel the same way *all* the time. From anger to reason to confusion to uncertainty to joy, sometimes these emotions pass through us in rapid succession. Cumulatively these moments of change, from happiness to sadness, aggressiveness to avoidance, confusion to fear, anger to passivity, can add up to a more substantive transformational moment over time.

In the same way, a character who exhibits the same emotion all the time feels unauthentic and thus could be viewed by the reader as untrustworthy. More important, change in the character's moods and reactions and feelings and emotions makes a story come alive. Moving from inside the character to the external action rivets the reader's attention. A character's emotional changes within a scene give readers what they need to make the story their own: emotion in the moment.

CASE STUDY: *A SHAMEFUL AFFAIR*

The opening scene of Kate Chopin's short story *A Shameful Affair* begins as follows.

> Mildred Orme, seated in the snuggest corner of the big front porch of the Kraummer farmhouse, was as content as a girl need hope to be.
>
> [cut to paragraph three]
>
> From her agreeable corner where she lounged with her Browning or her Ibsen, Mildred watched the woman [pull the great clanging bell that called the farmhands in to dinner] every day. Yet when the clumsy farmhands all came tramping up the steps and crossed the porch in going to their meal that was served within, she never looked at them. Why should she? Farmhands are not so very nice to look at, and she was nothing of an anthropologist. But once when the half dozen men came along, a paper which she had laid carelessly upon the railing was blown across their path. One of them picked it up, and when he had mounted the steps restored it to her. He was young, and brown, of course, as the sun had made him. He had nice blue eyes. His fair hair was dishevelled. His shoulders were broad and square and his limbs strong and clean. A not unpicturesque figure in the rough attire that bared his throat to view and gave perfect freedom to his every motion.
>
> Mildred did not make these several observations in the half second that she looked at him in courteous acknowledgment. It took her as many days to note them all. For she singled him out each time that he passed her, meaning to give him a condescending little smile, as she knew how. But he never looked at her.

Scene Tracker: *A Shameful Affair* by Kate Chopin

SCENE (SC) OR SUMMARY (SU)	TIME AND SETTING	CHARACTER EMOTIONAL DEVELOPMENT	GOAL	DRAMATIC ACTION	CONFLICT	CHANGE IN EMOTION	THEMATIC DETAILS
Ch. 1, SC 1	Lunchtime	Condescending toward the farmhands	To give him a condescending smile	Farmhand crosses class lines	X	+/-	

The Change in Emotion Column for this short story received a "+/-" because the protagonist's emotion at the beginning of the scene was positive (she is confident and condescending) but ends in the negative (she is being ignored). If the scene had started out with negative emotion and had risen as the scene progressed into positive emotion, then the Change in Emotion Column would have received a "-/+."

Feel free to write the actual change in emotion rather than use the symbols. For instance: "She goes from ignoring to being ignored."

CASE STUDY: *ALL THE PRETTY HORSES*

The character shows no emotional change from the beginning of the scene to the end. However, this in and of itself creates tension—we wonder why he feels nothing after having seen the dead man laid out. In showing no change of emotion, McCarthy creates suspense and thus forces the reader to read on to find out why. Later we learn that the character does not show a lot of emotion, and thus this opening scene accurately portrays a man who keeps nearly everything inside.

In this example, we leave the Change in Emotion Column blank.

Scene Tracker: *All the Pretty Horses* by Cormac McCarthy

SCENE (SC) OR SUMMARY (SU)	TIME AND SETTING	CHARACTER EMOTIONAL DEVELOPMENT	GOAL	DRAMATIC ACTION	CONFLICT	CHANGE IN EMOTION	THEMATIC DETAILS
Ch. 1, SC 1	Just before dawn	Speaks the truth		View of dead man	X		

CASE STUDY: *THE SEA-WOLF*

The protagonist begins the scene in a confident manner. However, before long the stranger hints that, because of all the fog in the San Francisco Bay, things are amiss.

> He gave a short chuckle. "They're getting anxious up there."

Soon after, the boat the protagonist is traveling on crashes into another vessel. Fear fills the protagonist as chaos ensues.

Scene Tracker: *The Sea-Wolf* by Jack London

SCENE (SC) OR SUMMARY (SU)	TIME AND SETTING	CHARACTER EMOTIONAL DEVELOPMENT	GOAL	DRAMATIC ACTION	CONFLICT	CHANGE IN EMOTION	THEMATIC DETAILS
Ch. 1, SU							
Ch. 1, SC 1	Jan. Mon. A.M.	Blames others; intelligent; writer	Write essay	Stranger appears	X	+/-	

CASE STUDY: *WHITE OLEANDER*

The protagonist's dark mood does not change much throughout the scene. Thus we leave the Change in Emotion Column blank.

Scene Tracker: *White Oleander* by Janet Fitch

SCENE (SC) OR SUMMARY (SU)	TIME AND SETTING	CHARACTER EMOTIONAL DEVELOPMENT	GOAL	DRAMATIC ACTION	CONFLICT	CHANGE IN EMOTION	THEMATIC DETAILS
Ch. 1, SC 1	Nighttime, Santa Ana	Deeply identifies with mother; 12 years old; afraid; takes care of mother	Give mother comfort	Roof w/ mother	X		

CASE STUDY: *WHERE THE HEART IS*

The protagonist's emotion moves from miserable to hopeful and from low to high throughout the scene. Most important, how Novalee shows emotion and how she feels at the start of the scene—on the verge of desperation to go to the bathroom—is vastly different twelve pages later when the scene ends. She feels triumphant because not only does she convince her boyfriend to stop, he also gives her enough money to buy herself a pair of shoes to replace the ones that fell through the rusted-out hole in the car's floorboard.

Scene Tracker: *Where the Heart Is* by Billie Letts

SCENE (SC) OR SUMMARY (SU)	DATE AND SETTING	CHARACTER EMOTIONAL DEVELOPMENT	GOAL	DRAMATIC ACTION	CONFLICT	CHANGE IN EMOTION	THEMATIC DETAILS
Ch. 1, SC 1	In a car headed for CA	17 yrs. old; 7 months pregnant; superstitious about sevens	To use the restroom	Riding in a car	X	-/+/-/+	

CASE STUDY: *THE ADVENTURES OF TOM SAWYER*

We know without being told that the character has a change of emotion from the beginning of the scene, when he is hiding, to the middle of the scene, when he is being threatened with a switch, to the end of the scene, when he runs to freedom. The Change in Emotion Column receives a "-/-/+," because the implied emotion begins as fear of getting caught, moves to fear of getting whipped, and finishes favorably.

Scene Tracker: *The Adventures of Tom Sawyer* by Mark Twain

SCENE (SC) OR SUMMARY (SU)	TIME AND SETTING	CHARACTER EMOTIONAL DEVELOPMENT	GOAL	DRAMATIC ACTION	CONFLICT	CHANGE IN EMOTION	THEMATIC DETAILS
Ch. 1, SC 1	Fri. Aunt's house	T: Small, smart, fast, liar A: took in dead sister's son	Escape	Tom/Aunt trouble	X	-/-/+	

TRACKING YOUR STORY

In the Change in Emotion Column, plot the emotion at the beginning of each of your scenes with a plus or a minus sign depending on how the character is feeling at the beginning of the scene. Continue to change the sign as the character's emotion changes. If no emotional change occurs, leave the cell blank.

Change in Emotion vs. Character Emotional Development

Change in emotion and character emotional development are two distinct but equally essential elements present in every scene.

Take a look at the Scene Tracker and note how narrow the Change in Emotion Column is. Compare its width to that of the Character Emotional Development Column, where plenty of space is needed to record anything that has to do with the character through whom the story moves and breathes at each unique moment in time.

The Change in Emotion Column is one of the narrowest because little room is needed to show emotional change. Using plus or minus signs, or drawing simple arrows pointing up and down, will do. For your story, you need only note the positive and negative emotional change the character goes through in a scene.

Character emotional development changes as the character passes through the entire story, step by step toward transformation. Change in emotion is a more focused, but fleeting, emotional shift the character experiences as he passes through a scene. Change in emotion indicates the visceral reactions the character feels in the moment.

The change in the character's emotion does not have to be significant but it should attempt to create a change in the character. There are always exceptions, of course, in scenes where characters enter and leave unchanged emotionally by what happens. But as long as you look for ways to record a change in the protagonist's emotional level somewhere throughout the scene, then your chances of keeping the reader's interest increases. If you can't record a change, then the scene has done nothing to develop the character.

Without some sort of emotional change in your character, your story will become stagnant and you will likely lose the reader. Stories are living, breathing organisms, as is your protagonist, who must grow and change as he tries to get something in life, fails, and tries again. Each time your protagonist is knocked down, he must get back up and steel his resolve.

It is best if the protagonist is in worse shape when the scene ends than when it began. No matter how bad things get for the character, the situation can and should always get worse.

If you find that your protagonist is always happy or always sad with few definite changes in emotion, then perhaps you are like the writer who told me that in tracking her scenes she found her piece was "a rather dour story of a dour character." Armed with that realization, she began working on integrating a variety of emotions to show more of the protagonist's strengths and hopefulness.

Keep writing. Do not polish. Do not go back and start over. Keep moving forward. Write your entire book as a rough draft all at once. Do not show it to anyone. Do not worry about spelling or grammar. Just keep writing until you get to the end. Only then do you know what you have.

THE WRITER'S STRENGTHS AND WEAKNESSES

Do not worry if tracking the emotional changes within your protagonist is difficult for you. Most writers have strengths and weaknesses in their writing. For instance, many writers are particularly adept at creating quirky, likable protagonists who feel emotions strongly, but those same authors have difficulty creating dramatic action and lots of conflict. Other writers are just the opposite and can create all sorts of amazing action scenes but break down when it comes to developing characters and their emotional growth.

Whatever your strengths and weaknesses, be aware of them. When you are feeling brave and energetic (if you were tracking yourself, you would receive a +), spend time in the arena you find most challenging. When your energy is low (you would receive a -), stay in your area of strength.

If the +/- symbols are too confusing for you, just jot down some keywords for the emotions. What really matters here is that your protagonist does not remain flat but is emotionally affected by the tension and changes within the scene.

We experience mood swings, albeit fleetingly, in reaction to every conflict we face. Chart those emotional changes for your characters.

THE ROLE OF EMOTIONS

Emotions are what make us human. Changing emotions in scenes transforms a cardboard and predictable character into an individual who is both fascinating and real.

Emotion is the character's reaction or a response to his relationship with others. It is a natural, instinctive state of mind both tied to logic and also separate from thought. Understand the role emotions play in your character's progress and how his feelings have the potential to either defeat him or lift him up.

In the middle, as the obstacles become more insurmountable, the protagonist should exhibit conflicting emotions. Her emotions, when out of balance, cloud her vision and dull her perception. Her personal powers of perception and intuition shut down. Emotions color a message's true meaning, linger, and become heavy burdens. The keynotes for emotions often translate in chaos and confusion and turn to drama just as the crisis brings the character to her knees.

In the end, she learns to control her emotions. The difference in her emotional maturity from the middle of the story to the end demonstrates her level of change and transformation.

As you examine how the character's emotions change throughout a scene and how he shows those changing emotions, examine how the scenes move you emotionally. Do you feel the same having read the end of the scene as you felt when you started it?

Grow to appreciate all the layers of both light and dark emotions as you search for patterns of what provokes your characters, how it provokes them, and why.

One by one, the protagonist confronts his beliefs. In the end, he becomes aware of another way to act and react. Rather than pass every decision through his intellect or unconsciously react at the emotional-response, gut-driven level, he begins to emotionally anticipate each major relationship that spins the energy of his life in a new direction. He slowly begins to greet these key moments that inspire change with confidence and a belief in the miraculous. Suddenly he is willing to risk losing the person he has always been in order to integrate who he is becoming.

Chapter Twenty-Four

THE THEMATIC DETAILS COLUMN

Of the three major plotlines (the dramatic action plot, the character emotional development plot, and the thematic significance plot), the thematic significance plot brings meaning to the effect the two other plotlines have on each other. Even if you're just pre-plotting story ideas, it's never too early to begin thinking about the themes of your story and the meaning your reader will be left with in the end.

Begin by tracking the general theme(s) in each scene. Common story themes include the following:

- family
- relationships
- revenge
- jealousy
- rivalry
- betrayal
- love
- death

By the time you've reached the end, you'll likely experience that "eureka!" moment: "Oh, so *that's* what my story is all about." At that point, you'll be able to form a thematic significance statement that *sums up* your story's deeper meaning.

CASE STUDY: *THE STONE DIARIES*

Carol Shields begins her Pulitzer Prize–winning novel *The Stone Diaries* in scene.

> Birth, 1905
>
> My mother's name was Mercy Stone Goodwill. She was only thirty years old when she took sick, a boiling hot day, standing there in her back kitchen, making a Malvern pudding for her husband's supper. A cookery book lay open on the table: "Take some slices of stale bread," the recipe said, "and one pint of currants; half a pint of raspberries: four ounces of sugar; some sweet cream if available." Of course, she's divided the recipe in half, there being just the two of them and what with the scarcity of currants, and Cuyler (my father) being a dainty eater. A pick-nibble fellow, she calls him. Able to take his food or leave it.
>
> [cut to paragraph six]
>
> And almost as heavenly as eating was the making—how she gloried in it! Every last body on this earth has a particular notion of paradise, and this was hers, standing in the murderously hot back kitchen of her own house, concocting and contriving, leaning forward and squinting at the fine print of the cookery book, a clean wooden spoon in hand.

Scene Tracker: *The Stone Diaries* by Carol Shields

SCENE (SC) OR SUMMARY (SU)	TIME AND SETTING	CHARACTER EMOTIONAL DEVELOPMENT	GOAL	DRAMATIC ACTION	CONFLICT	CHANGE IN EMOTION	THEMATIC DETAILS
Ch. 1, SC 1	1905 3:00 P.M. July in a kitchen	30 years old; has a passion for cooking	Make Malvern pudding for dinner	Cooking	X	+/-	"Stale bread"; "murderously hot kitchen"

The opening scene continues for almost six pages, but these paragraphs are enough for our purposes.

The theme is the *why*—your reason for writing the story, what you want your readers to take away. The theme of *The Stone Diaries* can be summed up in the following words: "Beneath the surface of seemingly ordinary women lie extraordinary lives."

Shields opens her story with foreshadowing and tension by stating that the mother will take ill. Then, rather than jumping immediately into the cause of the sickness and what happens next, she backs up. By using ordinary details—a wife preparing pudding for her husband's dinner and her absolute passion for cooking—Shields effectively introduces the theme and tone of the story to come. She presents authentic details in the first paragraph of her story and thereby establishes what her story is about and what it is not about.

Note the Change in Emotion Column for this scene. Though Shields begins by telling the reader about the mother's illness, when we meet the mother in the next sentence, she is not yet sick. The mother's emotion at the beginning of the scene is positive in that she is doing what she most loves to do—cooking. However, by the end of the scene, six pages later, the mother is sick. Therefore, the scene ends in the negative.

Don't give up on a book you're writing until you finish at least the first draft.

CASE STUDY: *ALL THE PRETTY HORSES*

Cormac McCarthy uses many telling details to bring the scene alive and lend an air of foreboding: "floorboards creaked under his boots," "along the cold hallway," "guttered candlestub," "face so caved and drawn," "the yellowed moustache," "the eyelids paper thin." Although the character shows no emotion, "in the distance a calf bawled." Because the use of "bawling your eyes out" is common when expressing sorrowful crying, weeping, or sobbing, when the reader reads about a calf bawling, he consciously or unconsciously transfers the sense of sorrow to include the protagonist.

There are other details, however, that actually enhance the story's theme, which is:

"When a boy is coming of age and the only life he has ever known is disappearing into the past, that boy must leave on a dangerous and harrowing journey to claim his place in the world."

The thematic details are the portraits of forebears only dimly known to him and the death of his grandfather. Both of these details serve as a metaphor for the death of the only life this boy has known.

Scene Tracker: *All the Pretty Horses* by Cormac McCarthy							
SCENE (SC) OR SUMMARY (SU)	TIME AND SETTING	CHARACTER EMOTIONAL DEVELOPMENT	GOAL	DRAMATIC ACTION	CONFLICT	CHANGE IN EMOTION	THEMATIC DETAILS
Ch. 1, SC 1	Just before dawn	Speaks the truth		View of dead man	X		Portraits; grandfather's death

CASE STUDY: *THE SEA-WOLF*

The theme of *The Sea-Wolf* is "Through ambition and courage, man is able to survive against all odds." In the first scene, the protagonist ends up in the freezing-cold water and fog with only a life preserver. Throughout the latter part of the scene, he shows panic rather than courage over and over again. This is an effective beginning in that the character has room to develop into a brave and ambitious man.

Scene Tracker: *The Sea-Wolf* by Jack London							
SCENE (SC) OR SUMMARY (SU)	DATE AND SETTING	CHARACTER EMOTIONAL DEVELOPMENT	GOAL	DRAMATIC ACTION	CONFLICT	CHANGE IN EMOTION	THEMATIC DETAILS
Ch. 1, SU							
Ch. 1, SC 1	Jan. Mon. A.M.	Blames others; intelligent; writer	Write essay	Stranger appears	X	+/-	Water like the grip of death; strangled by sea water

CASE STUDY: *WHITE OLEANDER*

White Oleander chronicles a troubled mother/daughter relationship. Its theme is "To find a place for oneself, one must first break away." Although the author does not use any thematic details to illustrate the theme, she does use ominous details to foreshadow the horror to come: "poisonous blooms" and "dagger green leaves."

Scene Tracker: *White Oleander* by Janet Fitch

SCENE (SC) OR SUMMARY (SU)	TIME AND SETTING	CHARACTER EMOTIONAL DEVELOPMENT	GOAL	DRAMATIC ACTION	CONFLICT	CHANGE IN EMOTION	THEMATIC DETAILS
Ch. 1, SC 1	Nighttime Santa Ana	Deeply identifies with mother; 12 years old; afraid; takes care of mother	Give mother comfort	Roof w/ mother	X		poison blooms; dagger green leaves

CASE STUDY: *WHERE THE HEART IS*

The theme of this novel is "Home is where the heart is." Novalee's long-term goal is to live in a house, any kind of a house. Up until now "she had never lived in a place that didn't have wheels under it." Therefore, by beginning *Where the Heart Is* in a car, Letts establishes right up front Novalee's reasons for wanting a house: The car is falling apart, and a TV tray covers a rusted-out hole in the floorboard the size of a platter.

Scene Tracker: *Where the Heart Is* by Billie Letts

SCENE (SC) OR SUMMARY (SU)	TIME AND SETTING	CHARACTER EMOTIONAL DEVELOPMENT	GOAL	DRAMATIC ACTION	CONFLICT	CHANGE IN CONFLICT	THEMATIC DETAILS
Ch. 1, SC 1	In a car headed for CA	17 yrs. old; 7 months pregnant; superstitious about sevens	To use the restroom	Riding in a car	X	-/+/-/+	Broken-down car; rusted floorboards

CASE STUDY: *THE ADVENTURES OF TOM SAWYER*

In *The Adventures of Tom Sawyer*, the theme is, "Man has a collective tendency to go overboard toward generosity and forgiveness." Aunt Polly embodies this theme in the first scene, but there are no thematic details to illustrate the point. Therefore, we leave the Thematic Detail Column blank.

Scene Tracker: *The Adventures of Tom Sawyer* by Mark Twain							
SCENE (SC) OR SUMMARY (SU)	DATE AND SETTING	CHARACTER EMOTIONAL DEVELOPMENT	GOAL	DRAMATIC ACTION	CONFLICT	CHANGE IN EMOTION	THEMATIC DETAILS
Ch. 1, SC 1	Fri. Aunt's house	T: Small, smart, fast, liar A: took in dead sister's son	Escape	Tom/Aunt trouble	X	-/-/+	

⟶ TRACKING YOUR STORY

With your Scene Tracker in front of you, refer to your manuscript and fill in under the Thematic Details Column any and all thematic details in each of your scenes.

The first time you fill in your Scene Tracker, you may not have worked out the theme of your entire project yet. For many writers, the theme does not reveal itself until the first or second rewrite. Therefore, if you do not have a theme, fill in the column with general details and do not worry about details that focus specifically on theme. Plot any details in the first passage that contribute to the overall meaning of that passage or to the entire story. List sights and sounds, smells and tastes, textures and details of your story's setting. List language details true to the time, such as slang and vocabulary. Attempt to use only the details that reinforce the character, the action, and/or the theme of your story.

In important scenes that turn the action of the story in a new direction, try to incorporate all five senses. Sensory details pull readers into the story in a way that allows them to move from thinking about your story to *feeling* it. The sense of smell generally evokes the strongest visceral reaction from readers. Use details for emphasis, but do not pile them on excessively—as in all things, balance is key.

Hang a list of the five senses–smell, hearing, taste, sight, touch–next to your computer as a reminder to integrate all of the senses into your scenes.

Once you are aware of your theme, return to the Scene Tracker and mull over each detail, searching for inspiration. Sometimes transforming a bland, trite, or stereotypical detail into an original, specific, authentic one imbued with thematic meaning is easy. But often it is a stretch and involves a shift in perspective.

Imagine your story as becoming a classic and read in the future, and attempt to use specific details that are authentic to the time period in which you are writing. For instance, in the first scene of *The Adventures of Tom Sawyer*, we read: "There was a slight noise behind her and she turned just in time to seize a small boy by the slack of his roundabout and arrest his flight." The roundabout is an authentic and specific detail of the time period in which this story takes place.

By tracking the thematic details in each of your scenes and seeing them hanging on the wall in front of you, the Scene Tracker becomes visual proof of how many scenes support your theme and how many stray away from it.

As we explore theme, you will begin to have a deeper appreciation of how to more deeply develop theme through details.

Choosing the Right Details

In a private consultation, a memoirist related to me the beginning scene of her story with a body lying on the floor with her arms outreached. Though the scene started the story with a bang, it was bereft of details and thus was not exploited to the maximum. The author did have a theme: "Through self-exploration, one is able to reconnect one's divided soul." The body on the floor represented the protagonist, who was hollow inside but a comedian and a colorful presence around others. With some plot coaching, the author was able to create a more layered scene by including thematic details of a bright, beautiful painting on the wall and absolutely no furniture, details that served as a metaphor for the protagonist's life.

The change in this example is subtle; the room still lacks furniture, but adding the colorful paintings shows a deliberate choice in leaving the room mostly empty; it's not an oversight. Plus, the paintings are in sharp contrast to the emptiness and, therefore, reinforce the theme.

Rather than use clichéd, general, or stereotypical details, you must research for just the right concrete, definite, and specific ones. Try to always stretch for the most original, authentic details you can.

Janet Fitch, author of *White Oleander*, reported that her mentor, Kate Braverman, asked her once what a cliché was. Fitch replied that it was language that had been repeated so often as to be common. Braverman retorted that it is anything you have ever heard, even once. Fitch then set out to write her story using original language, metaphors, and details never before heard.

Write the first draft of your story without thinking about all these details. There will be plenty of time during a rewrite to mull over every detail.

If you would rather move on to the task of filling in your Scene Tracker, move to chapter twenty-six now. If you would like to learn more about theme, read on.

THEME AS A REFLECTION OF YOUR LIFE

If you are like me and find theme one of the more difficult aspects of writing a story, I suggest that you refrain from shying away from those things in life that are hard, and instead walk right into them. Take out your story and roll around in the pages for a few days or more. Stick with it, even if the rolling turns into a temper tantrum of flailing arms and kicking feet and moans of "I don't get it! I hate this stuff!" Feel the fire of uncertainty and insecurity, and then go even deeper.

Had enough? All right then! Stand up and brush yourself off. Close your eyes, and take a deep breath. Now another deep breath. Open your eyes. Feeling better? My hope is that, in putting yourself through the emotional wringer, you might have discovered a theme or two that's present in your life. Since our personal themes generally translate into our writing, by deeply exploring your own themes, you might find the energy of your story—the fire—and its theme. Once that happens and you have a sense of the big picture, everything else will follow.

REPEATING DETAILS

Search for just the right detail that supports the theme of your project. Use that detail repeatedly. Each time you recall it, you will be emphasizing your theme.

Philip Gerard says in *Writing a Book that Makes a Difference* that "plenty of strategies are available to the writer for giving greater weight and impact to the theme and connecting more powerfully with the reader." One such strategy is to repeat thematic details. In doing so you can emphasize certain details, jog the memory of your readers, and/or establish rhythm. Let me give you a few examples of each of these.

The Red Tent by Anita Diamant is a story of Dinah, a woman only hinted at in the Book of Genesis in the Bible. Let us agree, for our purposes here, that the theme of Diamant's story is that the red tent is where a girl learns what it means to be a woman. The red tent was where women gave birth and were then pampered for a month afterward, the place a girl entered when she began menstruating, and the place she returned every month thereafter. Thus every time the red tent is mentioned or referred to, it gives thematic emphasis to the story.

An example of how the use of repetitions can jog memory is found in Ursula Hegi's historical novel *Stones from the River,* which she wrote as an attempt to understand the part of the common man in Germany after the end of World War I and through Hitler's rise to power. Keep in mind that although the detail Hegi uses to jog memory is not specifically a thematic detail, she is reminding us of a character who repeatedly deepens the story's theme through his actions and inactions.

In chapter one, Hegi introduces Herr Pastor Schuler with a common, and thus universal, character trait.

> Already he felt the itch of his sweat on his chest and beneath his private parts, a sweat he detested yet was unable to restrain with anything except medicated foot powder that left bone-colored rings on his garments and a chalky trace of dust on the tops of his shoes.

In chapter three, she repeats this detail.

> When Herr Pastor Schuler bent and reached beneath the cuffs of his trousers to scratch himself, Trudi [the protagonist] noticed that the skin on his legs was taut and shiny as though the hairs had all been scratched away. Specks of white powder drifted from under his cassock to settle on the polished black tops of his shoes.

She calls up the image again in chapter seven.

> … the aging pastor, who had been getting thinner over the years as though—by scratching his scaly skin—he were wearing himself away, layer by itchy layer, until soon only his bones would be left.

And finally, toward the end of chapter ten, almost halfway through the book, his scaly skin again comes into focus.

> [The new pastor] wished he could ask the old pastor about [the] confessions, but his predecessor had died the previous year, his poor, scaly shell so dried out that it had barely added any weight to the polished coffin.

Through the repetition of the scaly skin detail, we are not only reminded of who the man is, but we also are placed in the specific moment in the story; all of us can relate to the physical irritation elicited by itchy, scaly skin. The author goes to great lengths to reinforce the theme of the story; she wants us to remember this man over the course of the first half of the book because she uses his actions to show how, little by little, he and the other villagers made concessions as Hitler became more powerful, until there was no turning back. It is precisely this simple detail of scaly skin that drives home the idea that, if such a man as a pastor could fall prey to such human failings, then the same thing could happen to the very people we know and love. Ultimately this theme forces us to ask if we could have made those same small concessions.

Hegi also repeatedly mentions a monthly chess game Trudi's father had attended since he had been a boy, one that had been going on for four generations. In this example, the use of repetition establishes a sort of rhythm to the story while reinforcing the theme.

> The men would take the chess sets from the birch wardrobe, sit down at the long tables, and play, their silence punctuated only by punched chess clocks and the clipped warning: "Schach"—"Check." The white tablecloths would ripple, stirred by the rhythm of restless knees. Gradually, as it got warmer in the room, they would take off their jackets and sit there in their suspenders.

The chess game sets a thematic rhythm throughout Hegi's story. By showing how this ritual changes during the onset of World War II, she demonstrates how a game that had been virtually unchanged for generations was tragically deformed.

I chose these brilliant examples of repeated thematic details with the firm belief that they came to their authors just like yours will come to you: through a lot of hard work and many rewrites. The search for just the right thematic detail will ensure that each new rewrite you undertake will give your story a sharper focus and greater depth. Even better, these sorts of thematic threads make the struggle to identify the themes you live your life by, and thus your story's theme, worth the time it takes you to discover.

INSPIRATION FOR THEMATIC DETAILS

Writers have a tendency to get stuck in their heads, focus on only themselves, and look inward rather than outward. They obsess about the stories they write to the point that they often miss the details of the world around them. If this sounds like you, try one of these strategies:

- Close your eyes. How many objects in the room you are sitting in can you describe in detail?
- Pull yourself out of a conversation you are having with another person and watch the interchange, as if watching a movie. Memorize the words the other person speaks. Note what she holds back and how she conveys meaning through nonverbal communication.
- Recount the last conversation you had. What did the other person say? Your answers, or lack thereof, may surprise you.
- Look at the details that surround you. What do they convey about where you are on your writer's journey?
- Consider what you can let go of, both tangible and intangible, to move nearer to whom you dream of being.
- Whenever you are not writing, pay attention to the world around you and what others are saying. Carry a journal with you and jot down notes of your observations. Tune in to the details of the natural world.

These strategies will help you get out of your head and produce gems for the theme, mood, and nuances of your story. Most of a writer's genius comes in the art of the finesse. How finely you craft your project before you let it go is up to you.

Chapter Twenty-Five

CREATING
A LASTING TAPESTRY

Congratulations! Having ventured through Part Two of *Writing Blockbuster Plots*, you have begun the process of tracking your scenes on the Scene Tracker.

For those of you who protested that this sort of methodical, organized approach to writing is counterproductive to the creative process and therefore not for you, the fact that you are reading this passage says that you chose to face your fear. The reward for doing that which you most resist is always life changing. Congratulations!

Continue to fill in the Scene Tracker one scene at a time until you arrive at the last date, the last action, the final moment of character growth or regression, or the last perfect thematic detail of your story. As you proceed, you may need to refer back to the Scene Tracker explanations. Be patient. In time, and with practice, the elements of scene will become second nature.

If, however, tracking every scene slows you down or becomes too tedious, adapt the techniques I present in any way that best works for you. Remember, this process is intended to support you in your writing.

One writer confessed that using the Scene Tracker was exhausting (emotionally and physically). For her, it was an hour or two of toxic colored-pen fumes and shoulder aches from writing on the wall. But when she was finished and could stand back and look at her chart, she was exhilarated. So many elements of her story— funny episodes, sadness, courage, the craziness of the 1960s—were not revealed until she charted it out and could see the bigger picture. The Scene Tracker enabled her to organize and make some order out of chaos.

Most writers find that tracking each scene on the Scene Tracker is helpful in terms of looking at the elements of scene in detail.

ANALYZING THE SCENE TRACKER FORM

Sit back and examine your Scene Tracker. See if you can discover the mysteries and gems that you were unable to detect when you were blinded by your words and phrases, paragraphs and pages of narration. The Plot Planner showed you one of the structures of your story: plot at the overall story level. The Scene Tracker shows you another: plot at the scene level.

Search the Scene Tracker for any gaps or holes you can tighten, any leaps you made in the characters' progress, or any failure that needs to be smoothed out step by step throughout the course of the story. Make notations on the Scene Tracker with sticky notes to remind you to cut that which is not contributing to the whole or to flush out that which you skimmed over the first time around.

Remember that these are merely guidelines. The intent is for you to vary the design in any way that best supports your story. If everyone planned and plotted in exactly the same way, we'd have a bunch of cookie-cutter stories instead of unique works of fiction.

The seven essential elements on the Scene Tracker not only deepen the scenes and the overall story, but the prompts they provide "liberate invention." Pablo Picasso believed that "forcing yourself to use restricted means is the sort of restraint that liberates invention. It obliges you to make a kind of progress that you can't even imagine in advance." The practice of tracking your scenes provides this sort of restraint, and, in the end, creates overall coherence.

Continue reading for help deciding which scenes to cut, which ones to rework, and which ones to keep. Emotional change and conflict are the two most critical aspects to good fiction and, though they are most commonly missing in the early drafts of a story, it is possible to crank up the tension and conflict and create more emotional change in subsequent drafts.

In every case where you find a blank box under the Change in Emotion Column or the Conflict Column, rethink those scenes.

Once you have your Scene Tracker in shape, if what you find there inspires you to begin one of the several rewrites that are in store for all fiction writers, go for it. At any point you lose your passion for the actual writing, spend some time plotting on your Plot Planner. Good luck!

USING THE PLOT PLANNER AND SCENE TRACKER TOGETHER

For those of you who examined your Scene Tracker and decided you need to actually re-envision your project, do not despair. The answers are right there in front of you; they are always lurking in our stories. The Plot Planner helps you locate them.

In the Plot Planner section, you learned how to plot your scenes and how to best maximize cause and effect. You learned how to develop a compelling character plotline with lots of emotional changes. You learned how to create exciting and dramatic action full of tension and conflict in your action plotline. And you deepened your understanding of the importance of theme when you studied the thematic plotline.

Now, with both the Scene Tracker and the Plot Planner in front of you, you are ready to use all of the techniques to create a richly detailed and complex tapestry, one with a bold border and a compelling body, a resilient heart, and an expansive spirit. And once this complex fabric is woven with words and images, you might just find yourself holding a blockbuster novel.

SCENES TO CUT, SCENES TO KEEP

Count the number of scenes you have listed. Use that number now in much the same way you did in chapter three to help you determine and test where the beginning quarter of your story ends and the middle begins, and where the middle ends and the final quarter story at the end begins.

Draw a thick black line across your Scene Tracker after the end of the beginning scene or the scene that represents approximately one-quarter of your scene list. Do the same thing after the last scene that represents the middle of your story. In other words, divide your story between the last scene in which the protagonist is preparing for the end and the scene in which she takes her first step toward her final ascent to her goal.

If you're using printed copies of the Scene Tracker template, bundle and staple together three separate stacks: all the scenes in the first quarter of your story, those that represent the entire middle of your story, and those that constitute the final scenes.

Now evaluate your scenes in each section according to your notations on the Scene Tracker. Your strengths and weaknesses will reveal themselves immediately. This technique also shows the holes in the logic of your story, or where your characters come up shallow and weak, or where the thematic thread breaks.

A skill that defines a good writer is the ability to know which scenes to keep and which ones to kill. By creating a Scene Tracker and a plotline for your story, you can better select those scenes that best advance the story you've been chosen to write and those scenes that, in the interests of the story, should be reduced to summary or— dare I say it?—cut completely.

Likely you've noticed that I wrote, "the story you've been chosen to write." Before you roll your eyes and dismiss this line as an "out there" concept, I would like you to take a moment to consider the reason I have included such a seemingly preposterous idea.

When writers honor a story as something beyond ourselves, we put distance between our egos and that which the story needs. In other words, rather than falling in love with certain passages, sentences, characters, or plot twists that we've spent hours laboring over, we can appreciate those aspects purely for the sake of the story.

A good writer knows that the success of a certain passage, sentence, character, or plot twist doesn't depend on the beauty of the writing or the cleverness in the plotting or the depth of the characters, although these things are important and sometimes even captivate the reader. A good writer knows that each line and element in each scene belongs there because it has a definite purpose in the overall scheme of things.

Writers who are detached from the stories they write seem better able to finish a short story, memoir, piece of creative nonfiction, or full-length novel with fewer rewrites.

Make your scenes work for you by incorporating a strand of each plotline into every scene. Pretend there are three doors in every scene, one for dramatic action, one for character emotional development, and one for thematic significance. Open each door, one by one.

- **DOOR 1:** Where is the tension?
- **DOOR 2:** What aspect of the character is developed in this scene?
- **DOOR 3:** How has the theme of the story been advanced?

A good scene progresses the dramatic action, the character emotional development, or the thematic significance. The truly great scenes do all of it at once. To continue in that vein, any scene that does not accomplish at least two of these key functions at once does not belong in the story. With your Scene Tracker in hand, evaluate your story honestly. Where are the holes in the logic of your story? Where are your characters portrayed as shallow and weak? Where does the thematic thread break? If you cut the scenes with no tension and the scenes with no emotional change, is the story better off without them? Yes? Then for the sake of the story, you know what you need to do. What if you combine a couple of insignificant scenes into one great one? Or you might summarize the action in these weaker scenes in a sentence or two. If you see yourself as the steward of the story, you will yield to its flow and do what is right. If you see yourself as the creator, then you will resist eliminating any scenes, period. The choice is yours.

If you choose to do what is right for the story, and ultimately what is right for your readers, you might feel the urge to weep over all the time and effort you have just lost by cutting scenes from the story. When you are finished moaning and wailing over the unfairness of it all, dry your eyes. You have made the choice to be a good writer and to put your story first. The story and your readers will thank you.

The ability to view the narrative as a separate entity, apart from ourselves, allows us to more effortlessly cut those scenes that don't add to the strength of the story. This skill saves us time and heartache, and ultimately makes us better writers.

GETTING CLOSER TO THE CHARACTER

People love to read stories to peek into other people's lives, even if the other people are mere characters in a book or movie.

One of my client's stories was filled with dramatic action. It was exciting and left me anxious to hear what happened next. The writer masterfully provided more and more compelling action—the wife mysteriously goes missing and the husband nearly gets killed—and he did so seamlessly through consistent cause and effect. The dramatic action plotline rose quickly and effectively.

Still, during our plot consultation, amid all the intrigue and mystery, suspense and fear, the characters became cardboard action figures who allowed the dramatic action to happen *to* them. The more exciting the action, the more the characters were ignored and the less I found out about how the characters, especially the protagonist, were affected by the dramatic action. Without the help of the character to draw me nearer, I found myself separating further from the story.

The writer and I discussed the importance of goal setting, both at the scene level and at the overall story level. The better a writer is at establishing concrete goals for his characters, the easier it is for him to keep track of the effects on the character as she succeeds and fails in achieving her goals.

Even by the end of our time together, I never found out why the protagonist is missing when her husband is nearly killed. Why? Because the writer didn't know either. The author never opened the critical door into the character on a deep, personal level and thus robbed future readers from the intimate bond of knowing.

The writer used the protagonist to advance the dramatic action plotline but ignored the character emotional development plotline almost completely.

Still, he had done the hard part. The story was written. The dramatic action propelled the story in fast and exciting ways. Once I pointed out that the characters needed to be affected by that action, he easily opened the necessary doors. By attending to what is behind each door, the writer's chances improve for bringing satisfaction to future fans by knowing the character even better than the character knows herself.

TEST YOUR FINAL PRODUCT

Once you have plotted your scenes on a Plot Planner and analyzed each one for the seven essential elements, it is time to test your final product before sending off your manuscript to seek publication.

- Does every detail, every word, every sentence, and every connection have thematic relevance to the meaning of the overall story?
- Does every summary lead to the action that follows?
- Does every scene detail contribute to the thematic significance and make the dramatic action and the character emotional development more believable?

- Is every action meaningful, and does it advance the plot?
- Does every scene contribute to the whole?
- Is the conflict rising throughout the story?
- Have you provided adequate suspense and excitement to keep your reader engaged all the way to the end of your story?
- Is your core conflict resolved at the climax of your story?

If you find you are able to answer yes to every question, then go for it. Shout it from the highest hill—you're finished!

part three
APPENDICES

APPENDIX I: PLOT PLANNER FORM

Above the Line
Scenes that show:

- power is somewhere other than with the protagonist
- tension
- conflict
- complications
- loss of power by the protagonist
- dramatic action and movement
- confrontations
- the action of the story turning in a new direction

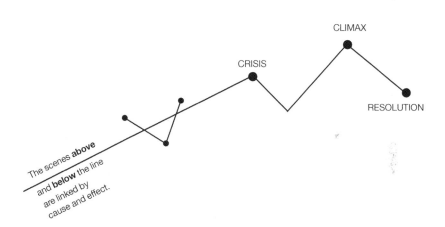

The scenes **above** and **below** the line are linked by cause and effect.

CLIMAX

CRISIS

RESOLUTION

Below the Line
Scenes that show:

- power shifting back to the protagonist
- introspection
- a lull in conflict
- the protagonist coping
- the protagonist planning

APPENDIX II: SCENE TRACKER FOR *THE ADVENTURES OF TOM SAWYER* BY MARK TWAIN

This Scene Tracker depicts the first two chapters of *The Adventures of Tom Sawyer* by Mark Twain. The theme of this novel is "Man has a collective tendency to go overboard toward generosity and forgiveness."

SCENE OR SUMMARY	DATE AND SETTING	CHARACTER EMOTIONAL DEVELOPMENT	GOAL	DRAMATIC ACTION	CONFLICT	CHANGE	THEMATIC DETAILS
Ch. 1, SC 1	Fri. Aunt's house	T: Small, smart, fast, liar A: took in dead sister's son	Escape	Tom/Aunt trouble	X	-/-/+	
Ch. 1, SU							
Ch. 1, SC 2	Fri. at dinner		Not to be found out/cut school	Interrogated	X (Will he or won't he?)	+/-/+/-	
Ch. 1, SU				Whistling			
Ch. 1, SC 3	Fri. evening	Not one to fight right away		Figure out new boy	X (Will he or won't he?)	+/-/-	Aunt forgave him earlier. Will he forgive new boy?
Ch. 2, SC 4	Sat. morning, field	Hates work Intro: J	To get out of work	White-wash fence	X (Will he or won't he?)	-/-	
SU				Painting			
Ch. 2, SC 5	Minutes later	Clever	Get someone else to do work	Ignores friend; friend falls for it	X (Will he or won't he?)	+/+	T.'s friends end up paying him to work

APPENDIX III: PLOT PLANNER FOR *THE ADVENTURES OF TOM SAWYER* BY MARK TWAIN

This Plot Planner depicts the first two chapters of *The Adventures of Tom Sawyer* by Mark Twain.

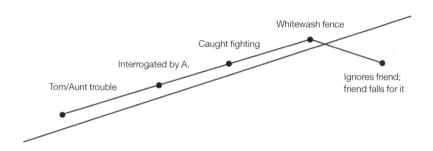

Scenes Above and Below the Line

- **Scene One and Scene Two** (chapter one) belong above the line because Tom, the protagonist, is not in control; his aunt is, at least until he escapes.
- **Scene Three** also belongs above the line because a fight ensues, and because of that, Tom is caught by his aunt, who has had enough of his antics.
- **Scene Four** (chapter two) belongs above the line because of Tom is not in charge. His scene goal, which is to get out of having to do his work, sets up tension with the question "Will he succeed or won't he succeed?"
- This same sort of tension continues in **Scene Five** (chapter two). We know Tom is clever, but no one is clever enough to convince a friend to do his work for him … or is he? The scene ends below the line because Tom *is* that clever. Not only is he clever enough to get his friends to do his work, they actually pay him to do it.

Cause and Effect

Scene one and scene two are linked because Tom's aunt is looking for Tom in scene one. Because of that, in scene two she finds him. Because she finds him, he escapes. Because he escapes he spots the new boy in town. Because of that, Tom gets in a fight. Because he fights and gets caught, he gets punished. And so on … .

APPENDIX IV: CHARACTER EMOTIONAL/ PSYCHOLOGICAL PLOT INFORMATION FOR *A LESSON BEFORE DYING* BY ERNEST J. GAINES

A LESSON BEFORE DYING BY ERNEST J. GAINES

THEME: "It is heroic to resist and defy the expected."

PROTAGONIST'S NAME: Grant Wiggins

OVERALL STORY GOAL: For Grant to impart his learning and his pride to Jefferson, a young black man who has been wrongly convicted of murder and sentenced to death

PROTAGONIST'S PERSONAL GOAL: To escape the quarter and marry Vivian

PROTAGONIST'S DREAM: To prove to whites that blacks are equal

WHAT STANDS IN HIS WAY? Grant's fear and secret, and Jefferson's resistance

WHAT DOES HE OR SHE STAND TO LOSE IF NOT SUCCESSFUL (RISK)? The respect of his aunt, Jefferson's godmother, his community, and the woman he loves

WHAT IS HIS OR HER FLAW OR GREATEST FAULT? His inclination to run away from conflict and unpleasantness or anything he might fail at accomplishing

WHAT IS HIS OR HER GREATEST STRENGTH? His intelligence and compassion

WHAT DOES HE OR SHE HATE? Plantation school, teaching, running in place

WHAT DOES HE OR SHE LOVE? Vivian

WHAT DOES HE OR SHE FEAR? That he will fail

WHAT IS HIS OR HER SECRET? That his mentor is right—that those who do not run away from the quarter will die a violent death or be brought down to the level of beasts

APPENDIX V: THE BEGINNING OF THE PLOT PLANNER FOR *A LESSON BEFORE DYING* BY ERNEST J. GAINES

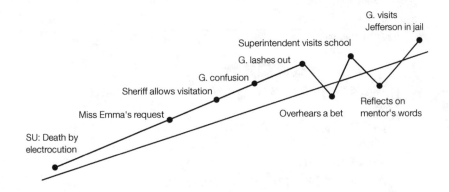

G. visits
Jefferson in jail

Superintendent visits school

G. lashes out

G. confusion

Sheriff allows visitation

Miss Emma's request

Overhears a bet

Reflects on
mentor's words

SU: Death by
electrocution

The Beginning of *A Lesson Before Dying* by Ernest J. Gaines

The story begins in summary, establishing the overarching conflict: An innocent man is sentenced to death by electrocution. This causes Miss Emma's request, which in turn causes Grant's desperate wish to "get away from here."

When the sheriff agrees to allow Grant visitation rights with the prisoner, the stakes grow ever higher. Grant does not say yes, but he does not say no either. Vivian asks him to "go for us."

Because of the pressure that is on Grant, he lashes out at his students, which in turn causes him feel that what he does is worthless.

Grant overhears a bet. This causes him to ask himself if he is to act like a teacher or like "the n----- I am expected to be?" He takes back control and decides to help Jefferson die with dignity.

In the next scene, the white superintendent visits the school. Although the superintendent humiliates him, Grant waves goodbye as he is expected to.

In the next scene, Grant reflects on Jefferson, who sat in the same classroom just a few years ago. That causes Grant to remember his mentor's words.

In the final scene of the beginning, Grant visits Jefferson in jail.

The beginning portion of *A Lesson Before Dying* introduces the characters, establishes most of the protagonist's Character Emotional/Psychological Plot Information, introduces the theme, begins with an enormous dilemma and ends on a cliffhanger. The beginning ends almost exactly on the one-quarter page count of the novel.

APPENDIX VI: PLOT PLANNER FOR
THE GRAPES OF WRATH BY JOHN STEINBECK

BEGINNING (SETUP)
On the family farm, preparing to leave

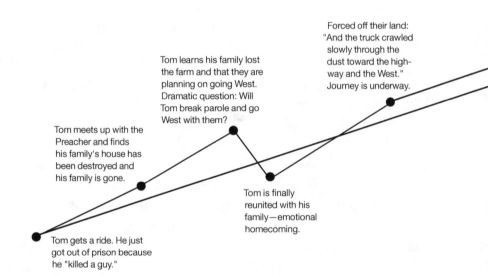

Tom learns his family lost the farm and that they are planning on going West. Dramatic question: Will Tom break parole and go West with them?

Forced off their land: "And the truck crawled slowly through the dust toward the highway and the West." Journey is underway.

Tom meets up with the Preacher and finds his family's house has been destroyed and his family is gone.

Tom is finally reunited with his family—emotional homecoming.

Tom gets a ride. He just got out of prison because he "killed a guy."

MIDDLE (MAIN ACTION)
On the road to California as family members
die or abandon the quest

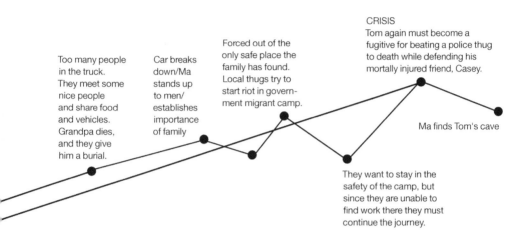

Too many people
in the truck.
They meet some
nice people
and share food
and vehicles.
Grandpa dies,
and they give
him a burial.

Car breaks
down/Ma
stands up
to men/
establishes
importance
of family

Forced out of the
only safe place the
family has found.
Local thugs try to
start riot in govern-
ment migrant camp.

CRISIS
Tom again must become a
fugitive for beating a police thug
to death while defending his
mortally injured friend, Casey.

Ma finds Tom's cave

They want to stay in the
safety of the camp, but
since they are unable to
find work there they must
continue the journey.

Download a larger version of this Plot Planner at
www.writersdigest.com/writing-blockbuster-plots.

END (FINALE)
In California, where the dream is revealed as a tragic hoax

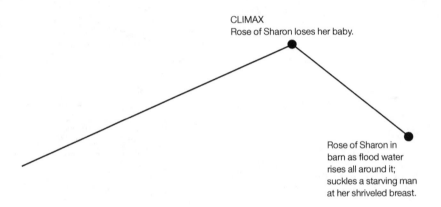

CLIMAX
Rose of Sharon loses her baby.

Rose of Sharon in barn as flood water rises all around it; suckles a starving man at her shriveled breast.

Download a larger version of this Plot Planner at
www.writersdigest.com/writing-blockbuster-plots.

APPENDIX VII: PLOT PLANNER FOR *THEIR EYES WERE WATCHING GOD* BY ZORA NEALE HURSTON

BEGINNING

(¼)

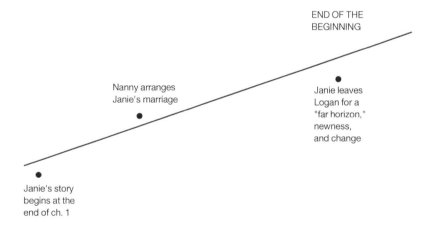

END OF THE
BEGINNING

Nanny arranges
Janie's marriage

Janie leaves
Logan for a
"far horizon,"
newness,
and change

Janie's story
begins at the
end of ch. 1

MIDDLE
(½)

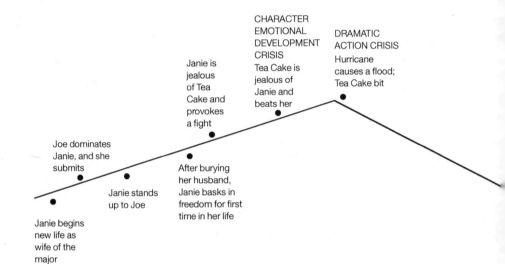

CHARACTER
EMOTIONAL
DEVELOPMENT
CRISIS

Tea Cake is
jealous of
Janie and
beats her

DRAMATIC
ACTION CRISIS

Hurricane
causes a flood;
Tea Cake bit

Janie is
jealous
of Tea
Cake and
provokes
a fight

Joe dominates
Janie, and she
submits

After burying
her husband,
Janie basks in
freedom for first
time in her life

Janie stands
up to Joe

Janie begins
new life as
wife of the
major

END

$(\frac{1}{4})$

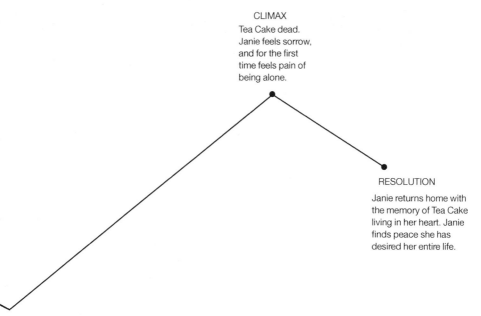

CLIMAX
Tea Cake dead.
Janie feels sorrow,
and for the first
time feels pain of
being alone.

RESOLUTION

Janie returns home with
the memory of Tea Cake
living in her heart. Janie
finds peace she has
desired her entire life.

Download a larger version of this Plot Planner at
www.writersdigest.com/writing-blockbuster-plots.

INDEX

development of, 31

emotional growth, 181, 182

getting closer to, 207–8

goals, 94, 163

internal aspects of, 95

introducing, 48

psychology, 180

relatability, 94, 181

secondary, 15, 62

strength of, 98, 103

transformation (*See* transformation, character)

Chopin, Kate. See "Shameful Affair, A" (Chopin)

circumstantial summary, 136

clichés, 197

cliff-hangers, 64

climax, 15, 22, 23, 29, 30, 43, 103

  antagonist's, 81–82

  Folly, 91–93

  plotting, 89–90

  and protagonist, 87–88, 106

complexity, 76

conflict, 4, 5, 14, 19, 22, 24, 28–29, 139, 169, 217

  and action, 169

  and cause and effect, 56

  and character flaws, 96

critical aspect of good fiction, 204

defined, 77

and flashbacks, 149

and goals, 97

intensifying, 84

introducing new, 77

in the middle, 63, 65, 76

plotting, 77–84

and scenes, 173

tips for creating, 179–80

Conflict column, 142, 174–80

confusion, 188

consistency, character's, 107–8

contemplative scenes, 72

continuity, sense of, 56

crescendo scenes, 76

crisis, 23, 28–29, 64, 65–67, 81–82, 103, 188

curiosity, 19, 51, 76, 169

dark night of the soul, 28–29, 64, 87

depth, 50, 155, 200

details, 56, 76, 139, 196–97, 198–200. *See also* Thematic Details column

dialogue, 169

dialogue, internal, 31

Diamant, Anita. *See Red Tent, The* (Diamant)

Dodd, Christina. *See Candle in the Window* (Dodd)

Doerr, Anthony. *See All the Light We Cannot See* (Doerr)

dramatic action, 4, 5, 14, 15, 17, 18, 20, 46, 50, 71–76, 94, 102, 139

  All the Light We Cannot See, 103

  in the middle of the story, 64

  vs. passive action, 71–73

  role in story ending, 120

Dramatic Action column, 142, 169–73

dramatic question, 62

dreams, 95–96, 164

driving motivations, 164

editing, final, 124

emotions, 62–63, 72, 83, 139, 188–89, 204. *See also* Change in Emotion column

ending, story, 29–31

  Candle in the Window, 34

  Folly, 8, 93

  The Grapes of Wrath, 220

  page count, 38

  plotting, 85–93

  role of dramatic action in, 120

  scenes, 37

  Their Eyes Were Watching God, 223

end of the beginning, 43–44, 50, 52, 103

energy, story, 23–24, 74

English Patient, The (Ondaatje), 147

episodic scenes, 54–56

expectancy, sense of, 71

Printed in the United States
by Baker & Taylor Publisher Services